MARY'S DIARY

A SECRET JOURNAL OF THE 1930s

Volume Three – 1937

MARY McINTOSH

THE PRESERVATION FOUNDATION, INC.
2313 Pennington Bend Road
Nashville, Tennessee 37214

preserve@storyhouse.org
http://www.storyhouse.org

Copyright © 2011 by Mary McIntosh.

All rights reserved.

Table of Contents

Chapter One – January 1937.............................5

Chapter Two – February 1937........................13

Chapter Three – March 1937.........................20

Chapter Four – April 1937..............................26

Chapter Five – May 1937................................34

Chapter Six – June 1937.................................42

Chapter Seven– July 1937..............................48

Chapter Eight – August 1937.........................57

Chapter Nine – September 1937....................67

Chapter Ten – October 1937..........................76

Chapter Eleven – November 1937.................86

Chapter Twelve – December 1937................93

Chapter One
JANUARY 1937

Mon. Jan 4 – Went over to see Mrs Barnicle & Gussie. Got back late & Mother was out looking for me. Got heck from Dad.

I can imagine how upset my parents were with my wandering around alone at night. Visiting in Pelham necessitated my taking a trolley there and back. While things were much safer in those days, it still would not have been smart on my part to be out alone in the dark.

Both my parents were sticklers for correctness in speech. Dad was especially strict about language. I never ever heard either of my parents use an expletive, or say anything obscene. I was being quite daring in what I wrote in my diary today. We were not even allowed to say "heck" as it was a shortened form of "hell." My daughter recently told me that when they were growing up I, too, insisted she and her brothers not use these terrible words. I guess it's true – the apple doesn't fall far from the tree.

Tues. Jan 5 – Margaretta & her grandmother came up to get me. Went to their house in Hempstead. Lovely house. chauffer, maids etc. Duck for supper

I don't remember this specific visit to Margaretta's grandmother's house., but I do know they would have come to New Rochelle to pick me up in a chauffer-driven car. They were very kind to me partly, I think, because Margaretta was somewhat a shy and retiring girl, and I was her only real friend at Low-Heywood. While we had our usual teenage spats and disagreements, we did stay friends throughout our school days.

After graduation we drifted apart, and just occasionally wrote to each other. I knew that shortly after our graduation she married, and was living in a small town in Virginia. Soon after graduation my parents moved to northern Massachusetts, where they remained for many years. However, because they were both getting along in years, and were feeling the cold weather, they eventually decided to try to find a house in a warmer climate.

I remembered that Margaretta and her husband were living in Virginia and recalled her telling me they owned a house they wanted to sell. I mentioned this to my parents. They visited the small town, fell in love with it and the house, and lived there happily for many years until their deaths. .

Wed. Jan 6 – We all had lunch at Schraffts. Had hot roast beef sandwich & swell ice cream desert. Saw "Stowaway" and "The Plot Thickens." Didn't do much in evening.

The day was a real treat for me. Rarely did our family eat at Schrafft:s, a well known but expensive restaurant during the Depression like Schtaffs was a luxury.

One of the reasons Margaretta and I gravitated toward each other was the fact that we both realized we were out of our normal pattern, mingling with the rich girls at Low-Heywood. Her folks were farmers, and her grandparents were responsible for sending her and her two younger sisters to Low-Heywood. After the first few weeks at school I never felt the rich girls looked down on me because I didn't come from a family that had the same amenities as they did. I hoped some of the reason was because I was liked. And too, the few times Dad came to the school and preached in the chapel, most of them thought he was great and so that reflected down on me. Margaretta, on the other hand, I think. often felt lonely and apart, though she was well liked by many.

I don't remember many of the girls touting their wealth. It was due, partly to the fact that even though these families didn't suffer to the great extent that many people did in the Great Depression, people still had to be careful in their spending.

So a meal at Schrafft's was a great treat for me.

Thurs. Jan 7 – Rained all day. Went round the village of Hempstead. Played games most of the day. Mr. Demerest gave me $1.00.

Many people who worked in New York City lived on Long Island. They rode the train in each day, as did those who lived in Westchester County. In all the jobs I had in New York, I don't recall anyone I knew who actually lived in an apartment in the city. During my tenure there, I resided at two different girls' clubs, which, like the YWCA, were very prevalent and inexpensive.

How pleased I must have been when Margaretta's grandfather gave me the munificent sum of a dollar. I could do a lot with that amount of money.

Wed. Jan 13 – Lovely day. Played basketball. Thought a lot about giving up Jim. Worse luck . Got a swell new gold watch from Dad. Strap too big though.

Why would my dad give me a new gold watch in January? Could it have been a bribe? Why would I make the comment about possibly giving up Jim on the same day I received a new watch?

Unfortunately I find I didn't write down my innermost thoughts as a teenager and so can now only surmise what transpired.

Father, in his wisdom had decreed I should give up the friendship with this young man, and apparently I was beginning to think along those lines. As it turned out it was physically impossible for me to carry on my great relationship with him because of our geographical constraints—he was sailing from Southampton, England to New York and I was ensconced in a girls' boarding school in Connecticut. But, for a while, I became as some of the other girls. I could tell them about the letters I received and the occasional phone calls I got, knowing deep down that my father would never allow anything permanent to come of this. And so I think, perhaps, the 'swell new gold watch' was given to me as a token of my dad's affection, and in gratitude for my agreeing to give up Jim.

But, what my father never knew was that Jim and I did get back together in New York during the war years when he was working for the British Merchant Navy.

Sun. Jun 17 – Church but no chapel. Rained all day. We all had a talking to from Miss Tilley & Miss Roper. Slept in afternoon

It was not often that the whole school received a lecture from our principal and vice-principal so I'm guessing a serious infraction of our rules must have occurred. These lectures, while few and far between, were always a little frightening, at least for me.

Some girls paid little attention to what was said. I always had thoughts of my father hovering in the background. If I received a "dressing down" from either Miss Roper or Miss Tilley, I would be sure I'd also receive one from Dad, and that would scare me more. Somehow he always found out.

Throughout my five years at Low-Heywood I'd had crushes on several teachers.

As most of them lived with us, they were there to help us when needed, not only with our school work, but also with our thoughts and ideas and problems.

Many of them were helpful, and I note on several occasions how kind they were and how much I loved them. But my favorite throughout these years was Miss Marjory Tilley, our vice-principal.

She was diminutive in stature, with a round friendly face, and wore rimless glasses. She never seemed to glide, as other adults I knew did, but walked rather briskly down the halls. Each one of us was one of "her girls." She was interested and concerned about all of us. Even on those days when I listened to a lecture from her, or was reprimanded for something I'd done, or omitted to do, I still loved her. She was my very special favorite and now, looking back, I realize she had a great influence on my future life and character.

Mon. Jan 18 – Rained most of the day. Played basketball. Margaretta & I didn't speak to each other until evening.

Tues. Jan 19 – Margaretta & I did French together. Read. Played basketball.

Wed. Jan 20 – Snowed most of the day. Played Basketball inside. Fell on the floor & hurt my thigh.

Not a very exciting three days – bad weather, poor relationship with my roommate and I fell and hurt my thigh.

Thurs. Jan 21 – Got into Honor Study Hall. Nasty day outside. Read.

I'm not quite sure I remember exactly what this Honor Study Hall was and the reason for it. Perhaps it was for those students who had pursued their studies diligently and were then given more free time instead of more study time, as had happened to me during my first two years

Fri. Jan 22 – Sewing. Social dancing. Read "Gone With the Wind." Wonderful. Went in Honor Study Hall for the first time.

Our library at school was well equipped, but I'm sure it wouldn't have contained a book such as GWTW. I tend to believe that one of the girls had brought it from home and it was passed around. I do know how fascinated I was with Scarlet and Rhett Butler, and how difficult it was to put it down and study hard for midterms which would be forthcoming shortly. I find I did not mention continuing reading GWTW, but I do recall that I grabbed it whenever I had some free time, in order to finish this wonderful saga of the South in the Civil War years.

Mon. Jan 25 – Had to go to bed early. Wrote my last letter to Jim. Our narcissus bloomed. Got a letter from Dad.

And so life went on—the "quick and the dead." I'd obeyed my father and given up my English boyfriend, no doubt a sad day. But there still was life—our narcissus bloomed!

My friendship with Jim was an unusual one. We'd only had a few days acquaintance on the "Georgic" last summer. I was 15, much too young to think seriously about him and, though I didn't realize it at the time, my life now was as an American. Too, I knew I had to obey my father. Alone I cried, and railed at him, for what he was doing to me, but in the long run I never, ever thought to defy him. It just wasn't done in our family.

As I look back now on this and similar incidents, I wish my father had left me alone to work out things for myself. What harm could a bit of letter writing across the Atlantic do? Was this a form of jealousy on his part? I'm sure in a few more years, I would have figured out for myself that if he lived in England, and I lived in America the chances of our ever getting together were mighty slim. But if my father had allowed me to continue to call him a boyfriend, it might have given me a self-confidence I was lacking at the time. As it turned out when we met again when I was in my 20s, he was just a friend, and, for a short time, a wartime lover. I had no regrets then that we'd never been able to continue our relationship through to marriage.

Sat. Jan 30 – Got my last letter from Jim.

Chapter Two
FEBRUARY 1937

Tues. Feb. 2 – Very cold & windy. Played Basketball outside. Got the nuttiest letter from Frank.

I was never as close to Frank as I was to Arthur, mainly because of the age difference. Frank had a dry sense of humor and I thought he was very funny. He loved to tease me. I am a "saver," and have boxes of "things" from the past. While writing this, I stopped long enough to dig through dry, brittle, brown papers I'd saved, and found this letter, dated January 29, 1937

He wrote me a long letter about finding bugs in our house on Elm Street. I quote part of it.

"About a month ago mother served some delicious chicken soup, and floating aimlessly on the surface was a cute little black bug. It was cooked to a turn and soup was oozing out of its ears...I gently fished it out and asked mother if she had run out of chicken and had put this in as a substitute...Last week we had turkey a la ex-king (the time was soon after Edward VIII abdicated), and on the side was a little heap of pure white rice. I was about to shovel a mouthful into the hatch when there was a little black bug perched on top of the rice just going into my mouth..."Mother, I have a bug in my rice." Mother apparently failed to understand me, for she said she would put the gas on and I could take a

bath later on…The hunt was on, we opened up the jar containing the rice and found no end of the cuties (or cooties) had taken up housekeeping in and around the grains of rice. I suggested we take some of them and train them to do tricks and save the rest for some other time when we had soup, but Mother had lost interest, and very callously it seemed tome, she drowned them and threw them out…"

It went on for another half a typed page, where he describes how they dumped out all the jars where the bugs might be living. He assured me that my food would be quite pure and wholesome when next I came home.

Thurs. Feb. 4 – Finished "Gone With The Wind." Wonderful. Nothing much happened.

I guess it would be a good to finish reading GWTW, a day when nothing much happened.

Feb. 5 – Had social. We went on a "sit down strike" for Mr. Hallowell to truck for us but he wouldn't.

I sat for a long time trying to remember what "truck" meant. Since Mr. Hallowell was our social dancing teacher, I assumed it was some kind of a dance, but I couldn't remember what kind. So, I sent an e-mail to Audrey, my friend I'd met during these years about which I am writing, and she told me what she remembered.

The dance was "trucking." One would hold their

finger in the air and move it and their feet moving in front of them by placing one foot hard on the floor and then moving the other one up. It was as if the person was waving a truck to make a stop and running up to get into it if it did stop. The song that was played while doing this dance was called 'Trucking Down the Avenue.'

When I wrote this notation over sixty years ago, I certainly never envisioned I would be able to glean what my phrasing meant by electronically asking a friend of mine, who lives across the country from me, what she remembered about it. I am so glad I have lived long enough to be able to use and enjoy the computer.

Sat. Feb 6 – Arthur & Louis came up to see me just as we were going on the walk. Only stayed a few minutes. They were on their way to college

"Hey kiddo," my brother said as I met them on the front porch of the Main Building. "How are ya? Louis and I thought we'd stop for just a minute to say hello. We're on our way back to college. Are you behaving yourself?"

"Of course she is," Louis butted in. "She's your sister, isn't she? And don't you always behave yourself?" he said with a grin.

"That gives her a lot of leeway, doesn't it?" Arthur laughed.

Louis Little was Arthur's roommate and best friend, and I thought he was great. He was like another brother to me. He often spent time at our house as his family lived in Massachusetts and our place was so much closer to Trinity College in Hartford, where they were attending. He was my date at the Junior Prom. Soon after Arthur left college, I lost touch with him. I never felt romantic toward Louis. I think he was too much of a brother-image for that, but under other circumstances it wouldn't have been hard. He was so good-looking with a shock of curly brown hair, and a winning smile. I do remember, though, seeing a photo of him some years later, and he was completely bald.

Fri. Feb. 12 – Went home. Mother and I saw "Love On The Run" and "Hopalong Cassidy Returns." Read in evening.

Wow, what fabulous movies were shown in 1937 at the local theaters. .

Thurs. Feb. 18 – Got a letter from Audrey. She is going with me to New York. Wrote 5 letters. Had my posture picture taken. Got 75 in English for month. Learned 32 lines of Macbeth. Ugh!

Audrey and I spent many of my days off together. I would take the train from Stamford into New York and she'd meet me at a pre-planned place. We'd almost always go to a show, then have lunch, and often in the afternoon visit a museum. She was, and still is, a very good friend.

I don't remember having this picture taken, but I would imagine I disliked it immensely. I hated the posture classes I had to attend, and I'm assuming periodically we had our picture taken to see if we had improved or not.

Obviously I did not like memorizing Macbeth as much as I had "Gray's Elegy in a Country Churchyard." I do not remember any of the lines from Macbeth, but I can still say a few from the Elegy. On one of my visits to England as an adult, I took a tour, which included the churchyard about which Thomas Grey wrote, and I actually sat under the tree where he penned it.

Fri. Feb. 19 – Social dancing. Played basketball in the afternoon. What a game! Had fun with "Slimy" in afternoon telling her the facts of life.

Tues. Feb. 23 – M.B.S, & I told Tigh & Pat Cole the facts of life. Heard that a bad rumour had gone around the school. Feel pretty awful about it.

Each of these must have been quite a session. Wonder where I suddenly learned so much about sex? Certainly not from my family, and I believe M.B.S. (who was Margaretta, my roommate) probably knew less than I did.

"Did you hear what some of the girls are saying about you?" Evelyn Tigh said later that day.

"What do you mean? What rumors are they spreading?" I timidly asked her. "Did you tell them what Margaretta and I were telling you? You promised you wouldn't."

"Cross my heart and hope to die," Evelyn said.

"Maybe it was 'Slimy.' She's got a big mouth. The rumor is that you have a dirty mind and maybe you have already 'done it.'"

For a moment I wondered if the rumor came from the faculty, and not the girls. I think it unlikely it would have been any of the teachers, for I'm sure I'd have had to report to someone. So it was probably worse for me that other girls were talking about what I was telling them. Living as close to each other as we did, it was almost impossible to be secretive about anything. I am just surprised that I felt I knew enough about this forbidden subject to be able to relay it to a couple of other girls. I'm guessing I was showing off and trying to prove to myself that I knew as much as some of the other girls. I never heard anymore about the rumor, but I was very careful after that not to talk too much about sex. I preferred to sit and listen.

We had no formal classes on sex education, not even any health-related lectures. In those years, these kinds of things were left for the family to inform their daughters. The only sex-related subjects we might have would be in biology and how a plant reproduced.

Sat. Feb. 27 - Took my Saturday with Audrey. Went to Grenfell party. Quite good. Saw "Last of Mrs. Chenny." Very good. Saw ice show at Rockefeller Center.

Even though Audrey was not as interested in Dr. Grenfell's missionary work in Labrador as I was, she had taken the same class with me at the summer young people's conference where we met. She was willing to go with me to this special occasion. I really don't remember what the occasion was, but I'm guessing it might have been a fund-raiser. Every so often I received a card or letter from Miss Cushman, secretary of the Grenfell Association, and she had invited me to attend this function.

We were allowed to leave school right after breakfast on our Saturdays off. A teacher would always accompany us to the station, purchase our ticket, and wait until we boarded. These expenses were deducted from the $100 our parents had deposited with the school. It took at least an hour to get into New York by train, but somehow Audrey and I always managed to cram a lot into that one day we had together.

Sun. Feb. 28 – Church & chapel. Slept a bit in afternoon. A man came to lecture & show slides on politics. Not so good.

Most of the visiting speakers the school planned for us were good, but occasionally we'd get one that was extremely boring. No matter, we had to sit quietly and act like we were listening and enjoying it. As a sixteen-year old, politics would not have interested me at all.

Mon. Feb. 29 – Not Leap Year

Chapter Three
MARCH 1937

Mon. Mar 8 – Got a letter from Isobel asking me to be bridesmaid. Excited.

Frank and Isobel had finally decided to get married. They'd been going together for a couple of years. Isobel was from Nova Scotia, and ended up being the only member of our family who never became a U.S. citizen. I never did learn why this occurred. This was becoming an exciting time for me, for it would be the first wedding in our family, and I was going to be a part of it. They planned to get married in April.

"Frank and I would like you to be a bridesmaid at our wedding, along with my best friend Annie. Would you like that?" Isobel asked later in person.

"Oh yes. I'd love to. I was a bridesmaid at my Aunt Phyll's wedding in England when I was just 10, but this will be more fun as I'm older," I busted out with excitement.

"You'll be shown what to do. Mostly it's walking down the aisle ahead of me. You and Annie and I will have to go shopping one day soon and pick out the dress for you both to wear. They'll be identical."

She became the older sister I'd always wanted and was kind to this new kid sister she acquired.

Fri. Mar. 12 – We are starting a new system of marks.

Disorders for everything & merits are gained. 30 merits give extended time on weekends.

In the old system we received demerits only. Now, we'd still get scolded and given a "bad" mark for things like our appearance, being late for a class or an appointment, or being sassy, but the other side of the coin was that we'd gain merits for not incurring any, or few, disorders during a semester. These became most important, for with them we could stay away from school longer when taking our weekend or Saturday, and that was a big plus.

Wed. Mar 17 – Had to write a character sketch of member of class for English. Wrote on Kay Daly. Got 83 in Eng. Test. 3rd highest in class.

One of the few people I occasionally kept in touch with after graduation was Kay Daly Fricker. She was a day student, so we never were as close as those with whom we spent twenty-four hours a day. Several years after graduation, on a trip back to California from visiting my folks in Virginia, I had a layover in Atlanta where Kay lived. She came to the airport to see me and we chatted about the old school days until it was time for me to board the plane.

"Do you remember in Miss Moss's English class we had to write a character sketch of one of our classmates and I did one on you?"

"No, I don't. What did you say about me?"

"I haven't the vaguest idea, but I do know I got an 'A'

for it, so I must have said nice things about you, either that or I said the bad things well."

We both laughed. It was good seeing her again.

Fri. Mar. 19 – One of the day-scholars came down with scarlet fever. All had to have the dick test. My roommate went home because her family was afraid of S.F.

When I started this story I vowed that when I quoted my diary it would be exactly as I had written it, and today's entry is a good example. Obviously I meant we all had to have the Schick test, not the dick test! Writing this as a "very senior citizen," I find it amusing that in my teenage innocence of those days I inadvertently used a word that in later years came to represent a certain part of the male anatomy. I'm sure in 1937 I had no idea what I was talking about, unless, perhaps, I'd subconsciously picked it up in one of the "sex talks," we girls delighted in having.

Sat. Mar. 20 - Announcement made that we could all go home today because of scarlet fever.

Easter Sunday was only a week away, and I believe the school authorities adjusted our normal spring break this year to include Easter. During my five years at school, I rarely was home on Easter Sunday. Because our school year started so late in September, and ended early in June, spring break was contingent on those dates, not on when it was Easter. With the scarlet fever scare it made more sense to switch things around and give us our spring break earlier this year. I was ready to go home.

Sun. Mar. 23 – Easter day. Audrey, Miss Howe (like me) & Miss Skinner came for tea. Had fun with Audrey.

I have mentioned how much Miss Howe and I looked alike. I wonder now if we still do, that is if she is still alive. I have no idea who Miss Skinner was. I didn't realize, until I started re-reading my diary, how often Audrey visited us. We always got along so well together, and my folks really liked her. It is so nice that now, as octogenarians, we are still friends. Even though we live far apart, we still communicate by phone or e-mail.

Mon. Mar 29 – Helped Mother. Arthur taught me how to drive. Fun.

Even in 1937, learning how to drive was an important milestone. My folks never owned a car, but by this time Arthur had his own. I learned on a stick shift, as that was the only kind of driving used at that time.

"Okay, kiddo." Arthur said to me this day of my spring vacation. "Would you like your first driving lesson?"

"Oh, yes. Can I? Did Dad say it was okay?" I was always so conscious of not wanting to upset my father

"Yes. You're sixteen now and, even though you won't have much chance to drive with being away at school all year, it will be good for you to learn. Come on, get behind the wheel of my car and please don't bang into anything. I need it to get back and forth from college." Arthur was such a nice guy. I loved him dearly.

Arthur was very patient with me and showed me all the ins and outs of driving a stick shift, but I guess it wasn't enough. A few years later, when I was old enough to obtain a license, I remember I flunked the test because I rammed into the curb when turning around in a narrow street. "Oh, well," I thought. "I don't own a car, and anyway I don't know when I'll ever be able to afford one of my own."

I didn't get my first license until I was 38 years old. After graduation I moved to New York City, and few people who lived in the city owned a car. Public transportation was good, dependable, and only cost a nickel. Then I married an Army sergeant and we lived in Texas, Japan, Alaska, Arkansas, and finally settled in California. We had a car for a short time when in Texas and Alaska, but I never drove them. Mac insisted he should drive, and I should take care of the children. When we finally arrived in California and he was due to ship out shortly for a tour of Korea, I knew I had to procure a car so I could get around. Arthur's faithful driving lessons stood me in good stead, even though I was now driving an automatic. I had passed the test. Through a notice in the paper I read of a second-hand Ford available in the next town to where I was living. Called "The Red Head," a name some previous owner had scratched onto the back part of the car, it was maroon, not really red. I don't remember the price, but I'm sure it wasn't very much. I drove it back home though how I managed I'm not quite sure. It was a stick shift, and while I'd originally learned on a similar car 30years ago, I had forgotten how to drive one. On the five miles home, I kept stalling the car. It was most embarrassing. In any event, it served me until Mac came back from Korea the following year when, I believe, he purchased a later model car. The only new car we ever owned (we never seemed to have any money for 'nice' things) was the 1962 Buick we won at an Angles baseball game in Los Angeles.

Each year, at the end of the baseball season, the Los Angeles Angels, (as they were then called) held a drawing at the last home game. They were our favorite team, even though we didn't get to go to many of the home games. The top prize at this drawing was a new car, and Mac won it. It was very exciting. On Monday he asked a friend to drive him into Los Angeles to pick it up. However, our joy was short-lived, for he sold it later in the week. We both had cars, even though they were not as nice as a brand new one, and we needed the money to pay off some of our debts.

Chapter Four
APRIL 1937

Thurs. Apr. 1 – April Fool's Day. Mother & Arthur went to Astoria with things. I saw "One in a Million" and "North of Nome." Very good. Played cards with Frank in evening.

Frank and Isobel were getting married in a couple of weeks. They'd found an apartment in Astoria, Long Island. Since Frank didn't drive, never had and never did, Arthur offered to take some of their things out there for him. He couldn't accompany them as he was working, whereas Arthur was on spring break from college. Frank and I rarely played cards together, so that was a special time for me.

Sun Apr. 4 – Church. The banns were read for Frank & Isobel.

The reading of the banns, for three weeks prior to a wedding, was obligatory in the Church of England. The American branch, the Episcopal Church, continued this practice, though few people bothered with them. My father had requested it, and so Frank agreed to have them read. They announced that these two people planned to get married in this church, and if there was anyone who knew of any reason why they should not, they should make it known beforehand.

Sat. Aug. 10 – Went to town with Beachy. Ate sardine sandwich & caramel nut sundae. Senior party – jungle. Quite good. Ate a lot. Felt whoopsee.

Now there's a word I like - whoopsee. I'm assuming it means I felt sick to my stomach, probably from all the garbage I'd eaten that day. I don't remember it being a common slang word for the times, and I certainly don't remember using it, but now as I write, it seems to fit in well.

Wed. Apr. 14 – Had to take sports & go to study hall. Arthur & Louis didn't call until 6:30. Arrived home. No rehearsal. Sat up & listened to Benny Goodman.

I was allowed to leave early because the wedding rehearsal had been planned for that evening, but had been called off. I did not know this until I arrived home.

In the 1930s teenagers were into swing music, and Benny Goodman was one of my favorites. I'm sure my parents, like parents of teenagers immemorial, did not care for the type of music we enjoyed. They tolerated it as little as I did the music my teenage children listened to in the 1960s.

Thurs. Apr. 15 – Got up at 9. Got a pair of white gloves. Went to Astoria & saw the new house. Went there & back in Louis car. Rehearsal at night. Frank got 3 cables from England. Bed at 11:45.

Of course I'd have to wear white gloves for the wedding. After all I was one of the bridesmaids and everyone, in those days, wore gloves at formal occasions.

Cables were the international telegram, and the best way to send greetings overseas. Few people in the 1930s had telephones, and I'm not even sure if there were many inter-country lines available. In any event, it would have been extremely expensive, and few of our family in England were in a position to send such a greeting. The cable worked fine

Fri. Apr. 16 – Frank & Isobel's wedding. I was bridesmaid with corsage of sweet peas & roses. Arthur best man. Went off lovely. Reception at Isobel's Chicken-wedding ice cream molds. Lovely cake. Sat next to Louis at table. He's wonderful. I like him a lot.

"Come on, Mary. Get out of bed. We've got a lot to do today. You can't be late for the wedding. Hurry up and get your bath over with so the rest of us can take ours. Your dress is hanging on the rack outside your closet door. I ironed it for you last night." My mother's voice sounded nervous. Perhaps she was. This was the first of her three children to get married, and it was a big day for her

Isobel was married in a two-piece beige suit, and wore a large straw hat, almost the shape of an upside down pie plate, decorated with a ribbon. She had on a large corsage of white gardenias and, of course, wore gloves. I had on a long brown coat and a flowered dress underneath. My hat was a little smaller than hers, and I think was also straw. Frank was dressed in a dark pin stripe suit.

I stopped writing long enough to search through a box of old photos I'd kept, and found some taken at the wedding. There was no color film for ordinary cameras then. I think we were still using an old Kodak box camera, though I do recall one I had which folded back into itself. But all these pictures were black and white.

There is a group photo of Frank and Isobel and the parents. Isobel's father was deceased. The hats both mothers wore were almost identical to the one Isobel had on—pinwheel type straw hats—and both had similar corsages. It was a chilly day, for they wore coats.

After the honeymoon they went to their apartment in Astoria, Long Island where they lived for several years, traveling daily into New York where they both worked.

When war broke out a few years later, Frank joined the Army. He was still a British subject, but was accepted into the Army because he had been born in a country that was an ally of the United States. Restrictions for being a U.S. citizen were lowered during the war years. However, this honor was bestowed upon him through the Army, and he became the first of the family to become a U.S. citizen. He was lucky. He didn't have to go through the agonizing question and answer period his sister had to do in a courtroom in New York City, on a hot July day, in a building with no air conditioning.

After the war he decided to stay in the Army, and one of his duty station was Ft. Dix, New Jersey. As I was now living and working in New York City, it was an easy trip for me to visit them. On a Friday evening in March of 1948, while at their place for the weekend, I accompanied them to the NCO Club. This is where i first saw, and met, Sgt. Horace Samuel McIntosh, who later became my husband. We all got along so well. They liked Mac, and their quarters gave me a place to visit, and get to know him better without many people being around.

Frank eventually became a warrant officer and retired after 20 years in the Army.

They bought a house in Newport News, Virginia. At this time I was living in California, so we didn't get to see much of each other. One day, though, stands out in my memory. It was right after my mother died in 1979. I had flown to Virginia for the funeral. The following day, mother's attorney asked the three of us, Frank, Isobel and myself (my brother Arthur was deceased) to come to his office for the reading of her Will.

Mother had left a Holographic Will, legal and binding as long as it was completely hand written, contained no witnesses, and there was only one copy in existence. The lawyer read this Will, and then gave it to Frank (co-executor with his wife). As Frank was 6'2" tall I couldn't read it over his shoulder, and I really didn't remember precisely what words it contained.

I learned later the Will stated that everything should be divided in thirds between Frank, Arthur and myself. However, Arthur had previously died and Mother had not altered her Will. I assumed everything would now be divided among the two of us. For reasons I never did understand, Frank discovered an obscure Code of Virginia that said that Arthur's children (now grown and married) would become the beneficiary in his place. I discussed this with a lawyer who thought differently. It turned out that with just the placement of a comma, a different interpretation could be made. At his recommendation, I had the Will read by a judge, who decided in my favor. I was to receive half of everything she had left, and Arthur's children would not be involved.

I was not trying to be greedy, but Frank and Isobel were childless, and Arthur's children grown and on their own. At that time I was raising four young children alone, with a very limited income, and so the judge's decision in my favor was such a great help to me. This did not make for a happy relationship between my only living relative and myself.

I did not hear from them again, until….

Frank died on September 27, 1980, which happened to be my 60th birthday. His wife did not tell me about this until a week later when I received a very curt letter from her. The letter started out "It is my duty to tell you that…" and ended by saying, "We, his wife and loved ones, were proud to stand tall for his Last Retreat."

I am now the only one left in my immediate family.

Sat. Apr. 17 – Got up at 9. Didn't have to come back to school until lunch. Rode back with Arthur & Louis. Open car. L. was simply swell. Alumnae game in evening. Went on hike. Very nice.

It was always fun when the Alumnae came back to participate in a game. Some of them I remembered, but often they would have graduated several years prior to my entering school. After I graduated I did return to the school a couple of times, but never to participate in an Alumnae game. My athletic prowess left much to be desired.

Tues. Apr. 20- Got pictures of the wedding. All very good. Very good one of Louis. Showed it to a lot of girls.

The good intentions I had of keeping Louis only as a special friend, another brother, seemed to have left me. I was so desperate for a boyfriend, and Louis was such a nice young man, that I clung to all the kind things he said to me. He really was very cute. I still have some snapshots of him in my special "black and white photos only" box.

I must have really enjoyed the fact I could show these pictures to my friends at school. Writing this memoir sometimes becomes a difficult feat. I am not one who easily succumbs to being weepy, but I often "hurt" for that young sixteen-year-old I used to be. How sad that I reaped such joy and pleasure out of pretending Louis was my boyfriend.

I'm sure I didn't show many pictures of other young men, for there weren't any.

Sat. Apr. 24 – Went on the hike. Played tennis all afternoon. Yale Glee Club came down and sang. Dance after. We couldn't go to it.

We always enjoyed it when the Yale Glee Club sang to us. I'm not too sure it was what they presented, how well they sang, or just the fact that there were a bunch of men standing in our formal living room. What a nice sight they were. New Haven was not that far from Stamford, and so it would be an easy journey for them to take. They were always so nice and polite, but I often wonder now if they really enjoyed their task of singing rousing college songs to a bunch of drooling, lovesick, schoolgirls, all dressed exactly the same.

I'm guessing the reason I mentioned the fact that there was a dance following the recital and we couldn't go was because it was probably only the Juniors and Seniors who were allowed to attend. If the Glee Club came down again to sing in a couple of years, I'd be a Junior and allowed to attend the dance. We might not see them again though, for I'm sure there were many other girls' boarding schools who would enjoy listening to them also. I think this was the only time they came to Low-Heywood at least while I was attending.

Chapter Five
MAY 1937

Sun. May 2 —Found out M.B.S. still feels the same way about me & told her mother all about it. She doesn't like me & I cried.

Oh, the trials of being a teenager when our hormones are raging. I wonder if girls still feel the same emotions as I did in those bygone days. M.B.S. was Margaretta, my roommate for many years. We loved and hated each other, depending on the circumstances of the day. But they were real emotions, and difficult to accept graciously. Perhaps the teenage years were a trial period for us all, a steppingstone into adulthood. I do know, though, that after she got married, and my folks bought their house, she completely ignored my family. One day, when Mother was walking down the one main street of this small town, she saw Margaretta glance at her, and then crossover to the other side in order to avoid having to stop and speak to her. I saw no reason for that occurrence. Even if she continued to dislike me in adulthood, there was no reason to take it out on my mother. After all, they had helped them out by buying their house. When I went home to visit my parents, I never encountered her, and before too long I heard they had moved to another part of Virginia. Maybe what she told her mother about me that day proved to be true

Thurs. May 6 - Saw the Hindenburg (zeppelin) in afternoon right outside of window & it crashed in evening.

Spring was in the air that Thursday, a day that breathed a promise of a verdant summer through the early opening of the redbud and the yellow forsythia, and wonderful smell of lilacs.

I was sitting in my bedroom, trying to study but not really very enthusiastic about it, when I glanced out of the window and saw the Hindenburg on its first transatlantic voyage of the season.

"Look, Margaretta," I exclaimed, "there's the Hindenburg. Miss Sparhawk had told us to watch for it, for she said it would follow the coast of Long Island Sound, on its way to its final destination in Lakehurst, New Jersey. " I'd love to go up in one of those some day, but I suppose you have to be very rich for that. Can you imagine being able to cross the Atlantic in such a short time compared to the two weeks it now takes on an ocean liner?"

"They scare me," she replied. "We're not supposed to fly like birds. That's why God gave us two legs to walk on."

I think she was serious, but I laughed and ignored her, and went on talking. "Miss Sparhawk said she'd read it carries only 36 passengers and a crew of 61, and that it is filled with flammable hydrogen instead of inflammable helium. Apparently hydrogen is cheaper."

I gazed at it again. It looked like a large white cigar slipping in and out of the clouds. It seemed to be traveling so slowly, but I knew it moved faster than it appeared. It would be nice to be up there in the midst of the clouds, I thought, and be able to gaze down on the earth below. Maybe I could even see my home in New Rochelle, for it would pass in that direction. I finally settled down to studying.

In early evening, Joan burst into our room without even knocking. "The Hindenburg got struck by lightning and crashed, and many were killed. Oh, it's terrible. It's on the radio in the Common Room. Everyone is huddled around listening to it."

We both dashed down the hall to the Common Room in time to hear the reporter, Herbert Morrison. He was sobbing. "Oh my God. The Hindenburg has been stuck by lightning at its mooring. Flames are shooting up everywhere. Many on board have been killed. Oh, my God. Oh, the humanity." This was the first news report to be broadcast nationally by the NBC radio network

I sat in silence, stunned. It was the first time I'd seen the Hindenburg, and with sadness in my heart I realized it was the last. I couldn't believe what had just happened. Why, I'd seen it just a short time ago, passing right in front of my bedroom window. The airship was gone, and for all those people who had died, it hadn't made any difference whether or not they were rich. I had tears in my eyes.

The great white ship had died.

Tues. May 11 – Nothing much happened. Washed my hair. Have to wake up a lot of people tomorrow morning.

Tomorrow morning was going to be the Coronation of King George VI and Queen Elizabeth and, because of the time difference between the east coast of the States and England, it would be on the radio at a very early hour. I had gotten permission to get up early, but it also meant a teacher would have to get up with us.

Wed. May 12 – King George & Queen Elizabeth's Coronation. Got up at 5. Heard the procession & all the ceremony, anointing, Communion. Wonderful. King George spoke in afternoon after an Empire broadcast. Felt homesick for England. God save the king! God bless them both! Vive le Roi.

How different life was then, with no television. From the verbal description we listened to, we had to depend on "seeing" it in our mind's eye. And how English I still thought of myself. Funny, I was now sixteen and had been away from England exactly the same number of years I'd lived there - eight. I think I was still very British for many reasons. All my relatives were still living there, and always did. None of them immigrated to America and, too, my mother and father kept an English household. We ate a lot of English food, we had Sunday afternoon tea in the living room on the round oak table that was one of their wedding gifts, we read English newspapers and magazines, and we talked a lot about England. I remember especially my dad was a great one for comparing things English and American. He'd mention different flowers in the States, such as the daffodils, which grew wild in England in the spring, and were a cultivated garden variety here. He'd compare the pronunciation and the spelling of words and sometimes how very different they were. They both loved America, but still retained so many English thoughts and habits. It took them many years before they became citizens, but I don't believe they were sorry they did.

Sun. May16 – Church & chapel. Mother & Dad & Elda came up. Swell to see them. Elda had to speak in chapel. They brought me candy, fruit, etc.

Elda, who became a missionary in China, was a friend of my father's. I loved her like an older sister.. She fascinated me because she was willing to go to that very far-off country in the world, where they dressed differently, spoke a strange language, and didn't look like anyone I'd ever come in contact with, other than our laundry man. And because she was going to do all this for God, I thought she was wonderful.

I still have a letter she sent me, incorrectly addressed, which was sent all the way back to China. Instead of sending it to 220 Elm Street, New Rochelle, N.Y. she had written 220 Elm Street, New York, N.Y. There were no postal area numbers in those days to help correctly direct a piece of mail. It is an interesting-looking envelope, with all the American and Chinese postal marks and stamps on it. It must have been opened, for on each end there is green paper tape with Chinese writing on it, but also in English are the words, "Post Office." I now wonder why it was opened, maybe because I don't see a return address anywhere on the outside. Apparently the Chinese authorities did their best to get it to the right person. It was somehow returned to Elda, and she sent it on to me, enclosed in another correctly addressed envelope.

Wed .May 19 - Horse show. Very nice. Worked on Biology topic. Mary Helen Drake has mumps & Jeanne Possett has measles. What a school.

With all the communicable diseases going around the school, I'm surprised more of us didn't catch them, including me. I'd had measles and chickenpox as a young child, but not mumps.

Each spring we watched the horse show at the Ox Ridge Hunt Club in Stamford. This was for those girls whose families could afford the once a week lessons, which cost $100 a year. It was always fascinating to me to see them on top of a horse in their riding habits, jodhpurs, boots, and a hat tied under their chin. Often I had to look twice to see who was riding. I knew that Ellen, in our class, was one of them.

Thurs. May 20 – Halo Fair today. Spent 50 cents on candy, etc. It was O.K. Had a lot of homework. One other girl has chicken pox.

The Halo, published three times a year, was the school magazine. The best work handed in to the English department was submitted to the Halo Board for consideration. During my five years at school, two of my submissions were printed.

In May of each year the Halo Board held a fair on the school grounds. We usually liked these, for it got us away from the everyday humdrum routine, even though I note that this year it was only O.K.

Sun .May 23 – Janeth and Patsy skipped church & were caught at it. Lot of hub-doo about it.

Mon. May 24 – The two who skipped church were expelled. Swell day.

Those in authority at our school did not fool around. We were indoctrinated early with the rules and regulations, and we were expected to abide by them or suffer the consequences. Attending church services each Sunday morning, and chapel on the school grounds each Sunday evening, were mandatory. As I write this I wonder how they thought they could get away with it, for I remember our names were checked off on a list as we boarded the bus to go to St. John's Church in Stamford. Somehow, I guess, they must have skipped out of line after the roll call occurred.

That was a pretty stiff penalty they received, considering it was only about three weeks before the end of school.

This is something that would never have entered my mind at that stage in my life. For one thing, I had been taught by my stern father to always obey my elders but, perhaps more importantly, religion was a very important part of my life, and I enjoyed going to church. I enjoyed attending chapel services. When, as a senior, I was appointed Head of the Chapel Guild, I considered it a great honor. At that time, I still had ideas of becoming a missionary someday.

But I smile at my entry "swell day." How incongruous.

Sat. May 29 – Freshman-Sophomore picnic. Fried hamburgers all afternoon. Willing Night. Got Henry doll & clothes. Soph went with Seniors for tree service & throwing of key into (?)). Very lovely.

Along with the Sophomores we, as Freshman, were hosts at this annual picnic, so frying hamburgers all afternoon would have been my job. In the evening, the Seniors came around to each room and willed objects to the younger girls. I have no idea what a Henry doll was. In early evening, before it got dark, the graduating class took the Sophomores on a traditional walk around a large elm tree on the grounds. However, I am unable to read where the key was thrown, or what the key represented. I just got up from my computer and tried to read it again but, since it is written in pencil and quite faint, it is impossible for me to read. It shall forever remain a mystery.

Chapter Six
JUNE 1937

Fri. Jun 4 – Class day. Very nice. Cup Night. A whole bunch of teachers on duty so we couldn't get into anyone's room. Had no food. Seniors kissed us goodnight.

As in most schools, Low-Heywood had established some traditions. Class Day, the day before graduation, the seniors willed tangible and intangible things to the juniors. At Cup Night awards for athletic achievements were presented.

One of the fun traditions we undergraduates always planned was a party after lights out. We assumed the teachers didn't know what was going on, but I'm sure they were well aware of what was happening and just looked the other way. However, this year we weren't able to sneak into each other's rooms to gorge on the forbidden food someone had managed to sneak into the school as teachers kept roaming around the halls.

Prior to this hoped-for escapade, the seniors went around to each of the undergraduates and kissed them goodnight. I liked this ceremony, for we didn't often have a one-on-one association with these older girls. Many of them I really liked and looked up to, for they seemed so sure of themselves. Hopefully I could be like them when I became a senior.

Sat. Jun 5 – Commencement. Went off swell. Chipped in with "Limy" & bought some roses for Betty Keifer. Mother & Audrey came up. Went to Garden Party for church. A Miss Meakam from Africa here.

Little did I realize when I scribbled each day in this diary that one day I would want to write about it. I think I was so used to things happening in a pre-ordained order that I didn't stop to wonder how Mother and Audrey came up to Stamford and how it was that I didn't stop to wonder how Mother and Audrey came up to Stamford and how I was going to get home with them. Mother never did learn to drive and, as a family, we never owned a car. I guess they took the train to Stamford and then possibly a cab to the school. If I'd only written more, it would have made it much easier for me to write this book.

I have no idea who Miss Meakam was, but I guess she was a missionary. As I still had strong inclinations toward this high vocation when I grew up, it would have been important for me to make a note of this in my diary.

Sun. Jun 6 – Church. Mr. Wilson's picture on front page of colored section of Times.

I met Mr. Wilson at the conference I'd attended two years ago. He was nice. I'd been able to talk to him about some of my questions and doubts about my religious beliefs, and so I felt a special kinship with him. I was unable to do this with my father.

Since he was the Rector of the church in Hyde Park, New York where President and Mrs. Roosevelt attended when they spent time in their home there, aeeing a picture of him in the Sunday New York Times was exciting.

Mon. Jun 7 – Hot day. Saw, "Romeo & Juiet" & "Counterfeit Lady." Very good. May possibly go to Mass at end of Aug. Jean Harlow died. Unpacked.

All the movies in the 1930s were double features, except in the large theaters like Radio City Music Hall in New York City where only one movie was shown followed by an elaborate stage show. In our local theaters, one movie was the feature, and the other second rate.

One of my favorite movie stars, Jean Harlow, who was often featured with Clark Gable, had just died, and this made me sad.

The possibility of my going to Mass in Aug. did not mean I would be attending a service at the Roman Catholic Church. Now I don't know why I even mentioned this and where I might be doing in Massachusetts.

Mon. Jun 14 – Hot day. Thunderstorm. Am meeting Miss Cushman for lunch tomorrow. Called her up.

One of the classes I attended at this conference was about Sir Wilfred Grenfell, a missionary doctor who spent many years working with, and preaching to, the fishermen of Labrador. I remember promising myself that someday I would try to do something as wonderful and noble as he had done, though I had no idea what or how I would accomplish it. In the meantime, I was very fascinated with his work, had joined the Grenfell Juniors support group, and kept in touch with Miss Cushman, the secretary of the Grenfell Association. Her office was in New York City, and on this day she had graciously agreed to meet me for lunch, along with my mother

Sat. Jun 19- Got Grenfell pictures from Miss Cushman. Started making screen. Went to high school & saw graduation. Saw Mr. Milos & Gussie.

I was into this Grenfell project. Mother found a folding screen she was no longer using, and I proceeded to glue pictures of the Grenfell Association and his work in Labrador all over it. I had no idea what I'd do with it when completed, but felt I was doing something worthwhile.

Going back to my old school for their graduation ceremonies was fun, but it seemed strange to see boys along with girls. How soon I had become acclimated to my new life-style. I saw Mr. Milos again. When I said hello to him, my stomach still did a bit of a flop, as I remembered how much I loved him when I was in 7th grade. I was proud of myself, for I behaved myself admirably.

Sun. Jun 20 – Mr. Taggard said I could see him next week.

Tues. Jun 22 – Called Mr. Taggard up but he couldn't see me until tomorrow.

Wed. Jun 23 – Called Mr. Taggard up but he couldn't see me. Worried about talk & what to tell Mother as excuse

Thurs. Jun24 – Didn't get to see Mr. Taggard at all. No one found out about talk etc. thank goodness. Prayed a lot to God about it. Got ready for conference.

 I find the comments for these four days very sad. Mr. Taggard was the Rector of our church. When I attended Sunday school there as a youngster, Mr. Haight was the Rector. We all loved him and thought he was great. It was through him that I was attending Low-Heywood. When he retired, Mr. Taggard took over. He seemed like a nice person, but I really didn't know him that well.
 I grew up in a family that didn't share our innermost thoughts with each other. I can only surmise that I wanted to talk with Mr. Taggard about some of my religious beliefs, questions I might have had about living a Christian life, and my hopes of someday becoming a missionary. I was only 16, and it was much too difficult for me to talk with my religious father or mother. I didn't want them to know these things. But how sad I sound when I worry about resorting to a lie in order to explain to my mother why I was going off by myself if this meeting had occurred.
 "Would you like to go back to the young people's

conference you attended a couple of years ago?" Dad asked me one day a few months previously.

"Oh, yes. Can I? That's where I learned all a about Dr. Grenfell and his work in Labrador."

Now I was getting anxious, for in a few days I would be returning. Maybe I'll find someone I can talk to about what is troubling me, I thought.

Fri. Jun 25 – Arthur drove me to N.Y.C. Got on bus. Lovely place. Wolves cabin. Walked from bus to camp with two girls. One Victoria friend of Audreys. Got settled.

I have no recollection of Victoria at all. Audrey and I met when I attended this same conference in 1935. We became close friends, and still are over 70 years later.

Sat. Jun 26 – Went swimming. Water nice. Met fellow called Ted Sloat. Had a talk with Mr. Greer. Good bunch in our cabin. Movies in evening, lecture & classes.

Sun. Jun 27 – Lecture & classes. Played ping-pong. Am getting good. Sang songs around campfire. With Ted all evening. Rained.

I had finally found a fellow who seemed to be paying attention to me and that made me feel good.

Chapter Seven
JULY 1937

Fri. July 2 – Took pictures. Packed. I really like Ted. He walked down to the Pavilion with me. After he left went roller skating. Felt sick on bus. Want to be back at camp with Ted.

    I was comfortable with Ted, and I liked the fact I had a boyfriend. I could go back to school in the fall and tell the girls about him. I would be on a par with them, I thought. I did not know then how soon that would all change.

Sun. July 4 – Dad arrived home. Had a long talk with him about Ted. Feel better.

    It is difficult for me to comment on what I wrote. I never remember ever being mad at my father. I'm sure I was annoyed at times, and I know I cried when he said things I didn't like, or told me to do something I didn't want to. I don't think even my friends got mad at their parents. It was just not the mores of the period, at least not in the circle of friends I knew.
    I don't remember what Dad and I talked about. It's possible he cautioned me about my relationship with Ted. In any event, having a talk with him, and listening to what he said I should do, or not do, doesn't seem out of place.

Wed. July 7 – Mother got the grippe. Had to do all the work today. Got "Death in the Rumble Seat" from the library. Pictures of conference came. One of Ted is very good. Gee, I miss him so.

Mother was ill with the grippe, now called the flu.

I wonder how many teenagers of today would take a book out of the library called "Death in the Rumble Seat." They wouldn't even know what a rumble seat was. We had friends who had a sports car with a rumble seat in the back. I remember once sitting in one with some fellow. Now I don't even remember his name, but it was supposed to be very romantic, and was a great place for holding hands and kissing.

Thurs. July 8 – Dad home all day. Interview at West. Comm. School. Probably land there instead of H.S

Dad and Mother had been talking about my needing some kind of skill so I would be able to support myself after graduation. It wasn't until World War II started that women began to branch out into realms other than the normal secretary, nurse, teacher, librarian jobs most women held. My family thought becoming a secretary would be an ideal job for me. Classes that trained us for these professions were not taught at Low-Heywood. It was mainly a college preparatory school. Even though I was attending there on a scholarship, I knew I wasn't smart enough to get a college scholarship. Only the rich families were able to send their daughters to higher institutions such as Bryn Mawr, Smith, Wellesley and other all-girl colleges. My parents decided that if I was able to type and take shorthand I would be capable of finding a job. And they were right. This is what I did during my working life.

The Westchester Commercial School was located in New Rochelle, so dad had me begin my training during this summer vacation. I don't remember how much it cost, but I'm sure it wasn't very much. Of course this is not what I really wanted to do, but I was still young, and my visions of becoming a missionary were far off in the future. I thought it was a good idea for, unless we went away somewhere, the summers were long. And, too, I was hoping I could meet someone there.

Sat. July 10 – Very hot day. Wanted to see Ted today but he didn't come. Quite lonely since I just hung around all day.

As I look back on those teen years, I realize the foundation for learning to be content with myself, was formed then. Granted I spent ten months a year intertwined with girls, but I believe that, too, had a lot to do with my being alone. I note here that I am lonely because I am alone. And I'm yearning to see Ted, who is, or perhaps isn't, my boyfriend. I never was quite sure how he felt. I believe during these formative years I learned to fend for myself and rely on myself. Despite the fact that there were often many lonely days, I was not often very lonely.

Mon. July 12 – Started sessions at Westchester Commercial School in shorthand from 8:30 to 1:30. Not bad. . A lot of work to do. Didn't meet anyone yet. Walked to Glen Island in evening. Cooler.

I attended this business school for just a few weeks, and managed to learn the basics of Gregg shorthand. I returned to the same school after graduating from Low-Heywood, and eventually finished the prescribed courses. It was a wise decision my parents made for me, though at the time I wasn't so sure, for being a secretary became my life's work, after circumstances forced me back into the working community.

Tue. Jul 13 – School. Cool day. No one has spoken to me yet. Quite lonely. Mother and I went to Symphony Concert at Glen Island in afternoon. M.B.S.'s grandfather died.

My personality at that time was not an out-going one. It would never have entered my mind that perhaps I should take the initiative and talk to someone first.
Margaretta's grandfather had been kind to me the day I visited them in Long Island, and I still remembered the dollar he had given me. I was sad that he had died.

Wed. July 14 – Went swimming with Mother. Ted called me up and then came down to see me. I knew he would. We played ping-pong at church & then sat & talked. Going to see him on Tues. Gee he's swell. Laughed a lot. Dad wasn't home.

Aha! Dad wasn't home, so Mother let Ted come down to visit with me. This entry intrigues me. If I remember, Ted lived in Harrison, a few miles from New Rochelle. But I'm wondering why we went to our church to play ping-pong. I suppose I felt it was a safe place and he wouldn't do anything inappropriate there. Also I don't recall any other place I knew where we could play ping-pong.

During these years, Dad was away a lot. He preached at various churches, and held spiritual retreats. Much of the raising of the three of us was left to my mother, though by this time the boys were old enough to take care of themselves. As far as my father was concerned, I was the only one who needed to be watched. I'm sure Mother didn't tell Dad what had happened, and who had visited me while he was away, and I certainly didn't volunteer any information.

Fri. July 16 – School. Hot day. Read (one line heavily inked out). Took test in shorthand.

I'm now intrigued by what I inked out. I have no idea what it might have been other than the fact that I either read somebody's mail that I wasn't supposed to, or a book that might have been banned. I think the latter is highly unlikely, for sexually themed books were not often written in those days, and certainly not kept in a library for public use. I would not have had access to books other than those my father purchased, or those I borrowed from the library. Most of the books in our house were religious-oriented. I remember sometime during this time-frame, I wrote a short piece titled "Father's Books," in which I mentioned that they were all of a religious nature, and therefore not that interesting to me as a teenager.

There is so much about this diary I now wish I'd gone into more detail. One of the reasons I didn't was that there were only four lines available each day, though there are some days when I crammed much information on those four lines. The other reason is that I was never one to communicate my deepest feelings and thoughts, and I am only now trying to resurrect them when filling in the days in this diary.

Mon. July 19 – School O.K. Got 100 in test taken on Friday. Nothing much happened. Started reading "A Woman Surgeon" for school.

Getting 100 in a shorthand test was a good accomplishment. Though I was currently only attending for a few weeks, I learned the rudiments of Gregg Shorthand in those early days. I can still write shorthand, though I don't have the speed I used to. When I do use it, though, I have difficulty reading it back. Once, some years ago, I discovered two Gregg shorthand books in a second-hand bookstore—the Anniversary Edition (which I learned) and a Gregg Shorthand Dictionary. They are fascinating now to look at. I wonder. Is shorthand taught or used anymore?

Since we were required to read a certain number of books during our summer vacation, "A Woman

Surgeon" was one of them.

Tues. July 20 – The Great Day. Ted came for me about 6:30. Picked up kids at Mamaroneck. Swell crowd. Ate supper. Saw fireworks. Went on roller coaster, ferris wheel, whip & others. 4 of us went on launch (another heavily inked out line). Got home at 12. T. is the grandest person. & not at all fresh.

I have to dig deep into my brain to remember all that happened on this day. Apparently my folks thought it was okay for me to go off with Ted for the evening. As I recall, a group of us who had attended the church conference together, planned an evening at Playland, an amusement park in nearby Rye, New York. Ted had arranged to pick up the others in his car. I have a feeling my dad was not at home when this all occurred, for I doubt he would have allowed this to happen. Mother was much more lenient and, perhaps, Arthur persuaded her that it would be okay. He was always sticking up for me. Again I find it fascinating that I inked out a few more words. My first thought was that Ted had done something on the launch, but then my next sentence says he wasn't at all fresh. However, do I really know what the expression "fresh" meant in those days? It might have alluded to being overly-sexual, instead of just trying to "cop a feel."

Wed. July 21 – Thought a lot of Ted last night. Went to Miss Peterson's for tea.

At least my father couldn't invade my thoughts about my boyfriend.

I'm sure my mother went with me to Miss Peterson's for tea. I wouldn't have wanted to go by myself. She was the spinster piano teacher from whom I took lessons, when I was 10 years old. I never liked her, and I didn't like playing the piano.

One day, on my way home from a lesson at her house, I was skipping along on the grassy part next to the sidewalk, happy that this lesson was over for another week. I did not like Miss Peterson, for she spit when she talked, and seemed to glare at me through the pinc-nez glasses she wore.

Suddenly I looked down aghast, for I had just stepped on a dead squirrel. My toes curled, my knees shook, and I ran home screaming, This incident left such a lasting impression on me that it was many years, and still is not easy, for me look at anything larger than a bug that is dead. It affected me so tremendously that when my mother was dying I did not go home to be with her—a decision I've always regretted, and which has stayed with me all these years. To help soothe my mind and feelings, I wrote a piece titled "Piano Lessons" in which I equate my fear of seeing anything or anyone dead with that day when I stepped n a dead squirrel.

I would not have enjoyed that visit with Miss Peterson.

Thurs. July 22 – Ted's birthday. Sent him a perfect card. Book of Birthday matches for his "stove-pipe". Mother, Dad & I had picnic supper on Davenport Neck.

We all teased Ted about the smelly pipe he smoked, which is probably why I sent him that card. It's a good thing my father wasn't reading my diary as it seems like every other day I mention something about Ted. Not sure he would have liked that.

Sat, July 24 – Went swimming at Glen Island. Read. Waited for Ted but he didn't come. Probably worried about family. Got letter from Beth. She said Ted had told the crowd he'd had a good time Tues.

Beth was one of the group I was with at the amusement park, though now I have no recollection of who she was. I assume Ted didn't show up because I'd warned him as to what my father was like, and that he should take it a little easy. .

Sat. July 31 – Hung around all morning waiting for Ted to call & he didn't but he came in afternoon. Vic & Andy couldn't come so just two of us went Didn't. go in water as it was cold & Ted had a cold Marvellous. time. Laid with head on Ted most of day Went to Hudson Park after. Ted said he'd miss me when I went away. Gee he's swell & I like him a lot.

What more can I say about a wonderful afternoon? I didn't know it then, but this was the last time I saw Ted. It was the end of my 1937 summer romance.

Chapter Eight
AUGUST 1937

Sun. Aug 1 – Went to church. Had 5 visitors for tea. Frank & Isobel left in evening. Nothing much happened.

As I look back and reminisce on those days, I often wonder how my mother put up with so much company. When she served tea, it was not just a cup of tea and a few cookies. She always produced a nice English afternoon tea, served on the round oak table, which sat in the middle of our sitting room. The tea included small sandwiches, sometimes watercress, potted meat, often jam or her homemade lemon curd. She might also serve scones and cake. The tea itself had been brewed the right length of time, and after pouring everyone present a cup, she covered the silver teapot with a tea cozy. Everything was delicious, always homemade, and gracefully served. No wonder five visitors came to tea. But as far as I was concerned, nothing much happened.

Fri. Aug 6 – Mother & I went to N.Y.C. In early afternoon & helped Dad at office & then in evening heard a symphony concert. Slept at office.

Occasionally Mother and I journeyed into the city and spent a night at Dad's office, where there were cots for us to sleep on. Sometimes I went alone and helped him with his office chores. I'd stuff envelopes and, occasionally, he'd let me file something. I guess he thought it was good experience for me, since I was attending a commercial school at the time. When Mother went with me, we usually took in a first-run movie or a concert.

Tues. Aug. 10 – Dad told me he had written to Ted telling him not to see me any more.

    Shortly after breakfast on that Tuesday I'll long remember, my mother told me she was going down to the cellar to do some laundry. She asked me to start packing for our trip, as soon as I finished washing the breakfast dishes
    I was about to go upstairs when Dad called to me to join him in his study. My guess was he was going to give me information about our forthcoming trip. The next day Mother and I would be joining him on a drive through New England. Along the way we'd stop at churches where the minister was on vacation. We'd stay in that area a couple of days. Dad would take the services and preach. Then we'd drive on somewhere else. It made a nice vacation for Mother and me, and I enjoyed going.
    I walked over to the sun porch where his office was—not as large as the one in Pelham, but it had a great view of the back garden. As I entered, he looked at me strangely, and told me to sit down. I couldn't figure out what was going on. He closed the door, and as he turned around I noticed that his hands were clasped behind his back. Somehow I had a hunch this conversation wasn't

about the impending trip. I couldn't remember anything I'd done lately that meant I had to sit here. For a few moments he said nothing, but I did notice his normally florid face was much redder than usual. I began to shake.

"I sent you to that church conference this summer because I felt it would be a spiritual experience for you. I did not expect you to fool around with some boy. I mailed a letter to this Ted person yesterday telling him I no longer want him to see you. Also, I don't like what you wrote in your diary about him. It's disgraceful. I don't want that filthy stuff in our house any longer. Either throw it away or cover it up."

"You read my diary?" I exploded. "That was supposed to be private. That's why I locked it. You had no right to read it, besides, we didn't do anything wrong." I sputtered, crying. "We didn't do anything wrong." I couldn't believe I was saying these things to my father. I'd never talked to him like this before.

"Throw it out or cover it up. Your choice," my father said as he started to open the door. "And I don't want you to see this Ted fellow again."

I ran up the stairs to my room, slammed the door shut, and threw myself on the bed sobbing. Why is he doing this to me? Why does he always make me change? I know Ted and I didn't do anything wrong. Why, oh why? I cried as I buried my face in my pillow. When I calmed down, I wiped my eyes and my nose. Then I picked up my beautiful red diary and hugged it to my chest. It was still locked, which meant he'd had to scrounge around to find the key, which I kept in the bag with my handkerchiefs. Now I needed to find another place to hide it. I walked over to my desk, found some white paper, scissors and glue and carefully, oh so carefully, I covered the four days he didn't like – June 28, 29, 30 and July 1, 1937. I could hardly see what I was doing as I started crying again. Tears rolled down my cheeks, but I quickly wiped them away. I didn't want them blotting out the new words I'd written.

As I wrote those last few words, I finally stopped crying. At that moment I hated my father, and this bothered me, for I'd been raised in the Christian concept of 'Honor thy Father and thy Mother.' I knew I'd probably eventually forgive him, though for the moment that seemed highly unlikely.

Many years later I tried removing the pasted on paper. Some of it came off, but most didn't. As a result it left ragged writing, which is now hard to read. This is what those four days now contain.

Mon. Jun 28 - Ted doesn't dance...with fellows

Tues. Jun29 – Lecture & classes. Gave our play. Pantomime...with Ted.

Wed. Jun 30- Went rowing with Ted. Ate in recreation hall.

Thurs. July 31 – Ted & I climbed up a mountain. I asked Ted if there were any wild deer in the mountains & he said "no, not wild ones." Chapel, lecture & groups...very impressive. Cried. Candlelight Service...

Ted, Vic, Andy & myself stood on dock for 10 min. arm in arm.

    The ellipses are where I couldn't read what I'd previously written.
    At the time I was very annoyed and upset. But it was not like me to defy my father. I covered the pages up, and this incident was never mentioned again. At the same time I heavily inked out something I wrote on July 12th and July 16th. I guess Dad missed these. Today, even I am curious as to what I wrote. I don't know if he ever read any more, but I was most careful what I wrote in my diary from then on. Later, after I started secretarial training, I wrote a few words in shorthand. I knew he'd never be able to read that! It tickled me, and it tickles me to this day, for even seventy years later, I can still read it.
    This intrusion into my private life stayed with me for years. At the time I didn't realize how devastating it had been. It was highly uncalled for, because I knew I had not written anything bad or sexual. And anyway, what right had he to question anything he thought I might have done. Wasn't his act of showing me his penis three years earlier far worse than anything I might have written in my diary? I know what kind of a teenager I was. I was much too religious to be doing anything out of line, and Ted and I were attending a church conference. Young people then, at least those in the circle of friends I had, did not indulge in, or talk about, "off-color" activities. The most that probably occurred between us was holding hands and kissing.

Because of this episode I swore, from that moment on. I would keep my most intimate feelings and thoughts to myself.

Wed. Aug. 11 – Started our trip. Saw friends off on the "Queen Mary." Grand boat. Saw 1st class rooms. Arrived at Stony Ridge, N.Y. at night.

I enjoyed seeing the First Class rooms, for when we sailed to England, we always went Tourist. Little did I ever dream that day on the Queen Mary she would later enter my life again in a very different way.

The waiter I'd met on the "Georgic," when Mother and I sailed to England in 1936, was a member of the British Maritime during World War II, and worked on the Queen Mary. Painted a battleship gray, she ferried American troops to England and, later, after peace was declared, brought British war brides to the States. I was working in New York in those days, and Jim and I got together when he was in port. When the "Queen" was no longer seaworthy, she permanently docked in Long Beach, California. It was on the Queen Mary that my eldest son had his wedding reception.

After our visit to this great ship, we started our trip with Thomas, one of dad's students, doing the driving. Not many women drove cars in the 1930s. This realm of driving was still delegated to men.

Sat. Aug. 14 – Left Lake George, N.Y. After breakfast. Arrived at Burlington, Vt. Dropped in to see Miss Sparhawk but she wasn't home. Visited Dog Team

Tavern – Grenfell. Very interesting. Arrived at Middlebury, Vt.

Miss Sparhawk was my French teacher in school, and I liked her. So the thought of being able to visit with her during the summer vacation was great fun. Unfortunately she wasn't home.

I was still very interested in the Grenfell Association and the missionary work Dr. Grenfell did in Labrador. I had read about this shop the Association maintained, and asked my dad if we could stop in to see it. He was agreeable. The shop was small, but fascinating, for it held souvenirs and mementos of his life in Labrador – small ivory walruses, bookmarks made of sealskin, books he had authored, photos of the mission and the people. I purchased a small walrus.

A couple of days had passed since my encounter with my father. I knew from past experience there was no point in whining or complaining. My father was his usual jovial self and didn't even acknowledge what had occurred. It was now a closed subject. I never told Mother what happened. I never told my husband what happened. I never told anyone what happened. Writing these diary entries is the first time I've remembered the circumstances.

What I find so sad is the fact that nowhere in the diary do I mention or describe what happened. I did write that Dad had sent a letter to Ted, and I believe that episode occurred on the same day, but I did not write about it. I wonder why. Was I so ashamed at what my father had done to me that I didn't want anyone to know? Was I devastated because the one person I looked up to and loved dearly had done such a terrible thing? Was I subconsciously trying to blot it out of my mind by not noting it in my diary? I do not know the answers to these questions. What I do know is that it did happen, for I have, as proof, the days in the diary where my original writing is covered up. I have sought, and am still seeking, professional help in removing the paper. However. Since it is over 70 years since the days in the diary were covered up, I think I will leave it as it is and not try to decipher what I wrote underneath. I know it was not bad. I know this day had a devastating affect one me because I became a very introverted person, afraid to say too much to anyone, or open myself up to my close friends, or husband.

Then I became a writer and discovered I could tell my story.

Thurs. Aug. 17 – Arrived at Littleton, N.H. Stayed at same cabins where Dad once stayed. Very bad thunderstorm in evening. A barn with 70 tons of hay & horse burned due to storm.

When we lived in Pelham and I was 10, I remember Dad seemed to spend a lot of time in bed. Mother told me he had bad headaches caused by his having been hit by mustard gas during WWI. I'd go upstairs to his bedroom and give him another cloth that had been soaked in vinegar. Apparently this concoction helped his headaches.

When he got better, his doctor recommended he go

away by himself for a little while Those were the days when he spent time in Littleton, New Hampshire, in the same motel where we were now headed.

Motels were not the elaborate ones of today. In those days, and for many years afterwards, they were not much more than small cabins strung together. The first motel opened in California in 1925 and cost $1.25 a night. Then, only twelve years later, we paid just $3.00 for a similar small room, with no amenities.

Thurs. Aug. 19 – Saw Arthur. He looks swell. Had lunch with us. Arthur & I went swimming. Arrived at Framington, N.H. Saw "The Good Earth."

For a couple of summers during the period covered by this diary, Arthur became a counselor at a boy's camp in New Hampshire. It was located on Lake Winnipesaukee. I always loved saying that American Indian name out loud. It was great to see Arthur again.

Fri. Aug. 20 – Arrived in Plymouth, Mass.

Mon. Aug. 23 – Rained all day. Mother & I visited the Antiquarian House. Very interesting. Antiques.

Tues. Aug. 24 – Walked all around Plymouth. Saw points of interest. Went a drive in evening. House across street robbed. Gorgeous sunset very red over water.

I enjoyed those days in Plymouth, and seeing Plymouth Rock where the Pilgrims first landed. A few yeas ago, I visited this city again and felt it still retained much of its original natural charm.

Mon. Aug.30- Thomas & I drove to Providence to get Arthur. Bus 1 1/2hrs late. Listened to Louis-Fan fight. 15 rounds. Louis won by points only

It was arranged that Arthur would travel by bus to Providence, when his camp closed, and we'd pick him up and all go back home together.

Listening to a world championship fight on the radio was something I enjoyed doing. Dad's interest was mainly in wrestling matches, and often just he and I would attend one in New York, but he agreed to join Arthur and me in listening to this boxing match. The three of us huddled around a small radio, without my mother being present. She was content to go off in a corner and read while her husband, son and daughter exposed themselves to such "barbaric events," as she called them.

Chapter Nine
SEPTEMBER 1937

Thurs. Sept. 2 – Arthur and I went swimming before breakfast. Got a letter from M.B.S. Family drove to Gloucester, Mass. Took the whole day. Played billiards in evening.

I have been to various parts of New England since those early days, but I don't believe I've ever covered it as thoroughly as we did on this trip. It was also nice having Arthur with us, for we always managed to do something in an evening, such as billiards. No TV in those days to while away the time.

M.B.S. was Margaretta Seymour, my sometime-roommate at school. At this point we were pretty good friends, and had been talking about rooming together again. What differences we'd had in the past seemed unimportant now.

Fri. Sept 3 – All went to Sturbridge Fair. Horse trotting & racing. Good. Long drive. Back at 10. Tired. Got a letter from M.B.S. Think we are rooming together.

It's looks as if our decision to room together was a mutual agreement.

Sat. Sept 4 – Went swimming in morning. Learned to drive. Drove thru park in afternoon. Played ping-pong

& beat Arthur one game 23-21.

I have a feeling my father didn't know what Arthur and I were up to, for I'm sure he wouldn't have appreciated the fact that I was learning how to drive. I was not quite 17, and certainly not an adult yet in his eyes. I took a driving test when I was 19, and flunked it because I couldn't turn around in a narrow street without ramming into the curb, and I never did learn to park well.

In those days a car wasn't as much of a necessity as it is today. After graduation I moved to New York City, where I lived and worked for eight years prior to my marriage. Then, as an Army wife living on military bases, the need for a car wasn't so important. We had cars, or rather my husband had them. We usually lost them because of his non-payment, or we sold them before shipping out overseas. The one I liked the best was a green Buick convertible we had when we lived at Ft. Hood, Texas in 1949. I don't remember what year it was, but it was not a new one.

After all Arthur's careful guidance, and because of the circumstances I've related, I didn't get my license until I was 39 years old. We'd moved to California, and Mac left for a tour in Korea. I had to have some kind of transportation while he was gone.

Mon. Sept 6 – Labor Day. Very windy & cold. Water sports – diving, swimming –baby beauty contest & fireworks in evening. Very nice day.

I have no recollection of this day, but I seemed to have enjoyed it very much. I hope, for the sake of the babies, that all these activities were held indoors

Tues. – Sept 7 – Left Plymouth in early morning. Drove all day. Picnic lunch. Arrived at Bennington, Vt. All saw Jane Withers in "Wild and Wooly." Swell.

Now that sounds like a humdinger of a movie; nevertheless, Jane Withers was a popular young movie star.

Wed. Sept. 8 - Drove through lovely mountains in Vermont & into the Berkshires. Stopped to see Mrs. Lawson but Edith was not there.

Mrs. Lawson and her daughter, Edith, were our cabinmates on the "Georgic" when Mother and I sailed to England last summer. I'm not sure if Edith and I had kept in touch, but I think our Mothers did. She was a couple of years older than I, and much more sophisticated and worldly-wise. I liked her, and was sorry she wasn't home that day.

Thurs. Sept. 9 – Drove around Mahopac. Arrived home in afternoon.

Fri. Sept 10 – Came up to Margaretta's. Nice place. Good supper. Nothing much happened. Arthur drove me up.

I remember spending this weekend with Margaretta's family on their farm in Ridgefield, Connecticut. It was a quiet place and what I needed after the turmoil of the previous afternoon. I did not tell Margaretta what had happened.

Her house and farm were a different life-style than I was used to. Her two younger sisters, Connie and Ida Read, also attended Low-Heywood, so I knew them, too.

Sat. Sept. 11 – Got up at 8. Gathered a lot of swell toadstools. Her friend Marion came down to sleep. The boarder Mr. Elvin took us for a drive & gave us ice cream which cost $0.35.

Wow! Imagine getting ice cream for four of us for thirty-five cents.

I recall that summer I was into studying toadstools and other fungi. Not sure what I would have done with those I picked for, I'm sure, eventually they would have shriveled up.

Sun. Sept. 12 – Went to Congregational church with M.B.S. & family. Very simple service. Arthur & Jeanne came & got me. They gave me a bushel basket of tomatoes & some corn.

It was Margaretta's parents who gave me the vegetables to take home to my parents. The way I wrote it, it sounds as if Arthur and Jeanne did.

Jeanne was Arthur's latest girlfriend, and I thought

she was wonderful. She was very pretty, and Arthur had met her in a special way

The previous summer Arthur, in the role as mentor to a young boy, had accompanied him and his parents to England. While on the ship he met a young lady named Jeanne. Since Arthur and the family traveled tourist, and Jeanne and her family were in the first-class section, this posed a problem.

All ocean liners had certain rules that passengers were expected to adhere to, one of which was that each passenger was required to stay within the confines of their own class. This meant that Arthur was not supposed to go into first-class. However, this didn't deter my brother, and somehow he managed to sneak over into first class so he could chat with Jeanne, and get to know her better.

After the trip, they got together again, and were friends for several months. We were very excited when we learned she was the daughter of Norman Thomas, the "forever, but never elected" Socialist candidate for President of the United States.

Mon. Sept 13 – Poured all day. Went to Rosemary Shearers. Did shopping for school. Got underwear, skirt, pajamas etc. Met Arthur. He drove us home Read. Frank for supper.

I'm guessing that I'd outgrown some of my old uniforms, and they needed to be replaced. I never did know how the financial situation of my five years at Low-Heywood was handled, I have no way of knowing if my parents were responsible for purchasing my uniforms. My tuition was fully paid; that's all I really knew. Even though these items would be inexpensive in comparison to today's prices, nevertheless they would have been an added expense. At least I remember the school didn't demand our underwear be identical.

I wonder if I enjoyed Frank for supper!

Wed. Sept 15 – Arthur went to college for day. Got a letter from Audrey. She's coming Sat. Mother & I saw "Married Before Breakfast" & "Talk of The Devil" in evening. Both swell.

As an adult one day I copied down all the movies I'd seen during these five yeas. I mention many of them now, for I find them a kaleidoscope of the cultural interests of those days. Most of them were flimsy, 'just-for-the-fun-of-it' pictures, but then there were also well known, and still well-thought of, movies such as "Captains Courageous," and "Gone With the Wind." Movies were a great pastime for, except for when attending a first-run theater in New York, they we all double features. We really did get our money's worth, since admission in an afternoon, when we usually attended, was $.15.

In today's world I would guess that a movie with a title such as "Married Before Breakfast" might be considered an 'R' rated movie, and who knows how bad "Talk of the Devil" was. But they must have been okay, as I said they were "both swell.:" In any event, there were no ratings given to movies in 1937. However, the

Hayes Office was in existence, and they would not have allowed any violent or sexual movies to be shown.

Sat. Sept. 25 – Met Audrey in New York. Saw "Lost Horizons" at Radio City. Marvellous. Had pictures taken. Toured News Building. Paper printed there. Saw some of Ripley's things at Macy's. Gave Audrey compact.

After Audrey and I became close friends, we made a pact with each other. If at all possible, we'd meet in New York on the Saturday nearest our birthdays. This was our Saturday outing. We continued these outings until Audrey got married.

Another thing we tried to do each year was to have our pictures taken. These would have been those taken in a photo booth, which seemed to be on almost every street corner and, which, I believe, are still in use today, though I presume cost more than the nickel we paid.

As I write of those early days, I smile at what I wrote. For many years I have said that there were two things I wanted to do before I died – ride in a stretch limousine, and go "skinny dipping." Added to that I'd often mutter that I'd like to see how a newspaper was printed, though that wasn't high on my list.

I got to ride in a stretch limousine on my 75th birthday, have not yet had a chance to go "skinny dipping," (naked swimming), but apparently I did get to see how a newspaper was printed. I wish I could remember what I saw, for if I went now, with computers in use, it would be much different than those days.

Mon Sept 27- My birthday. Left for school. Bill & Ruth drove me up. Nat's old room. Nice. A lot of new girls. Nothing much happened. Got lovely red roses (12) from Mother & Dad when I arrived back.

Certainly that was a different birthday, having to go back to school on that day,. I don't recall who Bill & Ruth were, but tend to think they were some friends of ours from church.

Here I go again. I'm now 17 on this day, a Junior, had a nice room that last year had belonged to Natalie, got a dozen red roses from my parents, but "nothing much happened."

Tues. Sept. 28 – School started. Have History, Math, English, French, Biol. Rainy day exercises.

Looks like a full schedule this year. I knew I had to do well, for there was only one more year left after this one. As I mentioned, Dad saved all my report cards. I just took a moment to look at what I had done in these subjects. I did very well.

Wed. Sept. 29 – School again. Got a book Called "'The Story of The Human Race." Fooled around.

Thurs. Sept. 30 – Played hockey. Lot of homework. Fooled around. Nothing much happened.

What did I expect the second day back at school, that

they would suddenly call a Wednesday a holiday? Brilliant writing "school again." Also, I seemed to be happy enough to be back as I "fooled around" both days, but again "nothing much happened."

EVENTS OF 1937

Howard Hughes flys coast to coast in 7 hours 28 minutes and 25 seconds. Beats his own record set the year before by almost 2 hours.

Huge flooding of the Mississippi and Ohio rivers. Thousands drowned or homeless.

A new house costs $4,000 or you could rent one for $26 a month.

A gallon of gas costs $.10

Edgar Bergen and Charlie McCarthy debute on radio.

"Gone With The Wind," by Margaret Mitchell receives the Pulitzer Prize in fiction.

"Snow White and the Seven Dwarfs", Disney's first full-length animated feature, opens to huge crowds.

World's first blood bank opens in Chicago.

Spam introduced – soon becomes the world's largest selling canned meat

Amelia Earhart and navigator Fred Noonan disappear over New Guinea. Never found

Chapter Ten
OCTOBER 1937

Sat. Oct 2 – Went on hike. Walked from New Canaan to school property. Had a picnic. Got toadstools and frogs etc.

Recently the school had bought a small piece of property in the New Canaan area. When we hiked, this often became a stopping off place for us.
I'm intrigued by the thought of my catching frogs. Did I really take them back to the school with me? And if so, I wonder how I kept them alive.

Tues. Oct 5 - Had a talking to from Miss Tilley because I scratched up the table in the library. I was the only one who admitted it though. I think she respected me for it. Miss Eyster told me I had improved very much in hockey.

After all these years, I remember this day very well.
A few days earlier, several of us had been in the library together and were chatting about classes, homework, missing our friends at home, etc
The school library was not large. On both walls were bookcases containing books, most of which were related to the classes we were taking, though some were just fun fiction. Two long wooden tables, with attached benches, were in the middle of the room. These were similar to a

picnic table in a park. However, these were larger and, we were once told, had been imported from Europe and had once belonged in a monastery. We were all aware of the historical value they held.

There were about five of us in the library that day. I recall I happened to have a protractor in my hand and, without really realizing what happened, I started scratching on the table with this protractor.

The next morning in assembly, before our classes convened, Miss Tilley spoke to the entire school.

"I am sad to have to report to you girls today that the monastery tables in the library have been marked up by someone. I have no idea who would do such a thing, because you all know how we value these tables. I do hope whoever did this will have the integrity to come and tell me." With just those few words, she left.

I did not go rushing into the office and admit my grievous error. I was not a saint. I was so scared of what might happen to me. Would I get a lot of extra time in study hall? Would I have to do extra duty around the campus, like picking up fallen leaves, even though gardeners were hired to do that? And, worst of all, if my father found out, what would he say? Would I be expelled from the school? I was scared, but I knew I had to admit to what I'd done, even though my actions were done subconsciously, and not with any great malice. I just wasn't thinking.

When I finally did report to Miss Tilley, she was very nice about it. However, she did give me a lecture on respecting other people's property, and then commended me on being honest enough to admit to it. She told me there was a mark also on the other table (where I had not been sitting), and apparently no one else had admitted to it.

I learned a lesson in honesty that day, one I've always tried to live up to and, which I hope, I passed on to my children.

The day wasn't a complete "wash-out." Miss Eyster, our gym teacher, told me I was doing better in field hockey. I was never very good in sports and so, when I did get a compliment on my accomplishments, it made me feel great.

Fri. Oct 8 - Miss Lee got a book called "The Romance of the Fungus World." Marvellous. Read about 100 pages. Had a lecture on Etiquette. Very good.

How fascinating that I so thoroughly enjoyed such a book. I must really have been into mushrooms, though I eventually did nothing about it. Science was never one of my better subjects

It's great fun reading and writing this diary, for I find a totally different ME than I am today. I somehow can't imagine a 16-year old girl of today admitting to enjoying a lecture on Etiquette. I'm sure in 1937, some of the rules of Etiquette were different than nowadays. Men held doors open for ladies, doffed their hats (which they always wore) when meeting a lady, and walked next to them on the side nearest the street. I learned once, though not in this lecture, that the reason for the man on the outside was that in the olden days women would empty their slop bucket by tossing the contents out of the upstairs window. If it landed on anyone, it would much more likely be the person nearest to the street. Also, before the days of the automobile, the streets would be busy with horses and buggies. Occasionally a horse might get scared and become skittish and, if this happened, it would be the man who would be in more danger.

Sun. Oct 10 - Church & chapel. Played the piano & hymns all afternoon. Slept in quiet hour. Study hall at night.

Our Sundays were always quiet. This didn't bother me for that's the kind of day I'd spent with my folks for as long as I could remember. I often wondered how many of the other girls resented so much Sunday discipline. I don't recall that many of us entered into sports on that day. We probably weren't allowed to do such great physical activity on the Sabbath, which also would require our donning our gym outfits. This would not be considered good Sunday dress or decorum. It was definitely meant to be a "day of quiet reflection." Re-reading this diary I was amazed that I was still able to play the piano. This skill was left from those days, a few years previously, when I trudged to Miss Peterson's house for lessons. I do recall, though, that I was not able to play much more than easy hymns.

And quiet hour meant just that. We were not allowed to visit other girls in their rooms, and were expected to keep our giggling or chatting to a minimum. As noted here, I usually ended up taking a nap.

I have in my possession the catalogue for the school years 1937-`1938, and what I've quoted is part of that written about Sundays.

"Sunday is observed as a day of rest and quiet when no visitors, except parents, are allowed. It is the purpose of the Heads to provide for the girls on Sunday the opportunities, none too frequently presented in the world of today, for quiet reading or letter writing, for walks along the shore or in the country, for thoughtful discussion or quiet meditation. Each girl is required to attend church in the morning and vespers in the school chapel in the late afternoon. For the rest of the day the program is flexible and the girls' activities, though under supervision, are largely left to their individual choice."

Oh, my! I didn't realize how "busy" the world was in 1937 that we were given few opportunities for 'quiet reading or letter writing.' In today's busy, busy computer-oriented world, I find this concept so fascinating.

Tues. Oct 12. Had a Russian singer in evening. Quite good but sang 2 hrs.

That was probably the understatement of the century – enjoying a Russian singer who sang much too long a time.

Fri. Oct 15 – Social dancing .Started playing ping-

pong tournament. Jean Faulkner beat me.

I had grown up in a family of ping-pong players. Frank, especially, was very good and often won tournaments, though it was usually Arthur who played with me. So when I entered the school tournament I felt I was probably as good as most of the other girls. I didn't win the first day.

Sat. Oct 16 – Played ping-pong with Miss McCarty in afternoon & Miss Metcalfe in evening.

Sun. Oct 17 – Church & chapel. Played ping-pong with Miss McCarty in afternoon.

Apparently ping-pong was considered a quiet enough game for us to be allowed to play it on Sunday. It was nice that the teachers were willing to play games with the girls.

As I glanced in the catalogue to see what subjects these two teachers taught, Miss Metcalfe/Math and Science, and Miss McCarty/English, I note that none of the faculty had a degree higher than a Bachelor of Arts, or a Bachelor of Science. I'm sure these were considered adequate requirements for teaching at Low-Heywood. I know that our school had a high scholastic rating, and most of the girls continued on at college after graduation. However, I believe the standards of college entrance were usually a person's grades through her high school years, and the taking of the College Entrance Board Examinations after graduation and before entrance. I remember that most of the girls in my class were studying very hard for these exams, which were considered the 'plum' for getting into the college of your choice. If you didn't pass them, you wouldn't be allowed to enter.

While I didn't go to college after graduation, I did eventually get a college degree. When I was 62 I received an A.A Degree in Liberal Arts, graduating with a 3.86 average, and receiving a gold rope placed around my neck by the Dean. I mainly went because I still remembered those days when I envied the other girls who planned to go to Smith, Vassar, Wellsley, Mt. Holyoke or other all-girls' colleges. Because I was working at the time, and had to attend at night, it took me five years to complete the two-year curriculum. But I did it, and did it well. Two weeks after graduation I hosted a party for all my friends. It was great, and an accomplishment I've always been proud of.

Tues. Oct 19 – Rained. Played hockey with A section. Miss Eyster asked me to. Got a letter from Frank who enclosed $0.25

That is not "a section" like any old section you could name, but it was the 'A Section' – the top hockey team. I was assigned to the B Team, so being asked by Miss Eyster to play on this day, was important. I'm guessing she thought since I had improved she'd give me a go at playing with the better team.

The school grounds were expansive. Behind the Main Building was a large field, religiously cut and kept neat for our field hockey games. At each end were goal posts. I occasionally glance at ice hockey games on TV, but notice that the players seem to be able to go anywhere on the playing area. We had to stay within our own boundaries, i.e. if I played 'forward' I could only run with the stick and round putt a certain distance, then I would have to flip the putt over to another member of the team.

This field was also used for lacrosse, since there was plenty of room to throw the ball among each other, while holding onto a stick with a net ready to catch the ball.

At the side of the field was a beautiful garden, with a white trellis, covered with roses in the spring. When the weather was fine, this is where the school graduations were held

How different our lives were seventy years ago. Getting a quarter from my brother was important enough to enter into my diary.

One thing that Low-Heywood did was to treat us all alike, no matter the background we came from. The fathers of several of the girls held very important business positions, often on Wall Street, but each of us was given the same allowance each week, depending on what grade we were in. I think it highly unlikely I mentioned the money that Frank had so kindly sent me. I might be trying to obey the rules, but I wasn't completely a "dunk-head." .

Tues. Oct 26 – Had English & Geometry tests. Got 93 in my geom. test. Second highest in class.

Wed. Oct 27 – Had biology test. Got 79 in it. Got 82 in English test

It looks as if I was beginning to do well in my studies. I don't remember ever being a "studious person." My goal, always, was to be sure I was doing well enough that my dad would be proud of me. As mentioned, I knew I would be unable to attend college, for financial reasons, but I also knew how pleased Dad would be, and he was, if I maintained a good average. And also, because I was not contemplating taking the college entrance exams, my classes were not the extremely hard ones, like Physics or advanced Latin.

Sun. Oct. 31 – Got a "special delivery" from Dad saying that Grannie died last Friday & is being buried tomorrow. Cried a lot. Called Mother up in evening. Halloween supper in Gym. Sang songs.

One of the most important forms of mail delivery in the 1930s was a letter being sent by "Special Delivery Mail." This was exactly what the name implied. It would be delivered in a 'special' way, in this case, I received it on a Sunday. Of course it cost more to send but, since regular letters were still only $.03, I doubt this would have cost too much. I wonder, though, why my parents didn't call me up to tell me. Perhaps they didn't know what a good time would be to reach me. I don't remember that they called very often, partly because the hours for receiving phone calls were restricted, and perhaps, too, because it would have been cheaper to send the letter this way than using the phone. If there was a cheaper way of doing something, my father knew it.

    Grannie was very special to me, as I'd spent all my summers when younger, with her in England. This was my mother's Mother. I did not know my father's mother that well and, in any event, they scared me for they were so religious it made religion not fun for me.

Chapter Eleven
NOVEMBER 1937

Wed. Nov. 1 – Went to chapel for about 5 min. silence at 9:30 - the time Grannie was buried. Got 92 in History test. Highest in class.

I wonder if I got permission to skip out of a class to go to the chapel, or if I just took off and explained when I came back. It would have only taken me a couple of minutes to get to the chapel, and it is quite possible this time coincided with a break between classes. But, too, I can see both Miss Roper and Miss Tilley saying yes to my request. They would have felt it was important for me to do this.

I was very fond of this grandmother, for my brothers and I spent a good part of each summer with her, when we were young. I remember my days with her—and it would only have been just a couple of months each year—more than I do of the other ten months spent in London. That proves to me how much I enjoyed being with her.

The highest mark in the class on a history exam was quite an achievement.

Sat. Nov. 6 – Went home. Arrived about 9. Shopped with Mother & bought a green felt sport hat. Fooled around most of the afternoon. Went to bed in evening.

When I started writing about this diary I was determined to cite my exact words, whether or not the spelling was correct, and whether or not any of it made sense. This is one example. Here I am getting the highest grade in the class on a history test, and I am brilliant enough to write in my diary "went to bed in evening." What an exciting thing to document, and for me to try to write about almost seventy years later!

I well remember the green sport hat. It looked a lot like what Robin Hood might have worn, and had a tall green feather, sprouting out at the top.

Hats, at least women's hats, were an important part of our wardrobe in those days. No one would think of going anywhere important without one. They were worn everywhere, in movie theaters and restaurants, on trains and to work, and especially when attending church. No one would ever dream of entering the holy sanctuary of a church without a hat, or something to cover ones head. Usually a new hat was purchased for Easter Sunday, often one with flowers around the brim. These hats usually had a veil, sometimes just a small one that covered only our forehead; others came down to our chin. The custom was to wear last year's Easter bonnet on Palm Sunday and a new one on Easter.

At school we only had two hats, the red beret we wore each day when it was cold, and the brown hat on Sunday to church. This hat is hard to describe as it looked a lot like a man's hat, sitting on top of our hair. None of us liked either one of these hats, so being able to shop on my Saturday at home and pick out one that looked like something that came from Sherwood Forest, was a great thrill.

Thurs. Nov. 11 – Armistice Day. Patsy Fox got expelled for smoking. Hockey. Nothing much happened. Started making a black & white design & initial mittens for Audrey.

I do not remember who Patsy Fox was, but I'm assuming she was a boarder. The Heads of School had little control over what the day students did outside of the confines of the school, but they were totally responsible for the boarders.

In 1937 people smoked everywhere – in offices, in shops, on trains, in movie theaters. My folks were dead set against smoking, and when my brothers were of age and started smoking, my Dad frowned, but said it was okay as long as they never smoked in the house. I just re-read the 1937-1938 school catalogue and nothing is mentioned about the ban on smoking. My guess is that at that time most young girls did not even consider smoking, especially if no one in their family did. It would, therefore, be important for either Miss Roper or Miss Tilley at the first school assembly each year, to announce to the girls the ban on smoking. It was a daring thing for anyone to do, as teachers always seemed to be lurking around a corner when you didn't want to run into one.

Most of us were knitters. It was something we could do without having to obtain too many extra things needed. As many of the girls, and teachers knitted there was always someone to help out when needed. I was busily knitting a pair of black and white mittens for my good friend Audrey. Wonder if she remembers them? Maybe I should send her an e-mail and ask. My, oh my, how our lives have changed.

Fri. Nov. 12 - Knitted most of the day on my mittens. Have nearly finished one side. Social dancing with a guest man teacher. Swell.

I wonder why this guest man teacher was so "swell." We did have a man come every other Friday night to teach us, so there must have been a special reason I mentioned this one. Perhaps he was better looking than our regular one; perhaps he was more willing to dance with the girls; perhaps he taught us some different steps. Who knows. But I seemed to have enjoyed him.

Sat. Nov. 13 – Poured all day. Lots of free time. Finished one mitten all but thumb & sewing it up. Rin-Tin-Tin picture in evening. Very exciting.

A day of having to stay within the confines of the school was not one we usually looked forward to. After an hour of study hall in the mornings, Saturdays were free. Sometime we went into Stamford with a teacher and were allowed to shop in certain stores only. Other times, those of us who belonged to the Hiking Club took off walking. When the weather was good, others played tennis. So a day of having to stay inside the school probably got pretty boring. Based on that I can perhaps surmise why I thought a Rin-Tin-Tin movie was exciting. I'm not sure, but I'm guessing it might have been a silent movie, for even though the school occasionally showed a sound-track movie, I'm pretty sure that most of the Rin-Tin-Tin movies were silent ones. And of course, in 1937, all the movies were black and white.

Wed. Nov. 17 – Nothing much happened. Hockey.

Thurs. Nov. 18 – Nothing much happened. Hockey.

The joys of living in a girls' boarding school!

Wed. Nov 24 – Had study hall from 1:30 –3:30 then went home. Arthur arrived about 7. Hiich-hiked from Hartford for 10 cents. Snooty slept with me. Didn't go to sleep until well after 3.

    Each semester we were allowed to be away from school for one Saturday and one weekend. However, we could only go home for Thanksgiving for the one night before, but had to return by Friday. Turkey and all the trimmings were given to those girls who lived too far away to be able to go home, or occasionally they could spend the day with someone who lived close by.
    I am so amused by the notation that Arthur hitchhiked from Hartford, Connecticut, where he was attending Trinity College, all the way to New Rochelle, New York and it only cost him ten cents.
    It was so nice to be alone in my own room at home and for Snooty to spend the night with me. Not going to

sleep until after 3, I imagine it was because "she" listened to my telling her all the tales of my life at school. She was probably used to it by now, for it was not easy for me to talk about my feelings and I rarely did so to my parents. Snooty, I knew, would always keep my secrets.

A year after my graduation when, because of unforeseen circumstances, it was necessary for my folks to move to Massachusetts I went with them, and Snooty traveled in an animal crate. A family friend drove us there. Mother and I spent the night in a hotel in awaiting the delivery the next day of our household goods. However, since my father had once read that it was extremely difficult for a cat to get used to a new place especially when it was empty, and that they could kill themselves by knocking their head into walls, he opted to spend the night with Snooty. He slept on the bare floor. When the furniture arrived, and she got the smell of familiar objects, she ran around the house and seemed to understand that this would be her new home, which it was until her death a few years later.

Fri. Nov. 26 – School again. Next series by Miss Erskin. Very good. Miss Roper's stomach rolled in the middle of it

I do not remember who Miss Erskin was, or what series she was giving. I just looked in the catalogue and she was not a regular member of our faculty, so I'm guessing she was a guest speaker who had presented a previous talk to us. What delights me about this entry is that I had the nerve to mention that Miss Roper's stomach made a loud noise in the middle of this presentation. Now, doesn't that sound like the thing a teenager of the '30s might have noticed? How much more sophisticated the teenagers are today.

Tues. Nov. 30 – Someone has stolen my Yardley's soap. I'm mad.

Now that's a serious offense. Any product from Yardley's was not cheap, and I'm sure this was a gift from my mother. I doubt I ever got it back. Our rooms were never locked, and any one could wander around and take things. We never had anything of any value because none of was allowed to wear jewelry, and any money that belonged to us was kept in the school office. But, we did have some personal things like shampoo and soap. I doubt this was returned.

Chapter Twelve
DECEMBER 1937

Fri. Dec. 3 – Had Geometry & History test. Left for home. Went shopping in N.R. New Arnold Constable store opened. Swell

In checking the report cards I have for that year, I ended up getting an A- in the History test, and an A in the Geometry. My dad would like those grades.

This would be a weekend I was taking. N.R. – better known to its inhabitants as New Rochelle – was a fairly large town, much larger than Pelham where we had lived. It included several main streets, and now that a new Arnold Constable had just opened, that meant that its image would be enhanced, for Arnold Constable's was an upscale store. We rarely shopped in those kinds, but it was fun looking around, especially since this was a brand new store.

Sat. Dec. 4 – Went to N.Y.C. with Mother. Went Xmas shopping. Did quite a bit. Met girls from school & saw "Fifty-fifty" – a play by some University of Penn. Boys. Very good.

New York' City in the 1930s was a safe place. Even though on this day I traveled with my mother and did some shopping, I was allowed to stay on and meet the girls from school. Mother probably took my purchases back with her and, after the play, I would get on the New York, New Haven & Hartford Railroad for the short trip back to New Rochelle.

Everything was so cheap then. We could eat a good lunch for fifteen or twenty cents, and busses and subways cost a nickel. I have no idea what this play was about - though the title now intrigues me – the names of the girls I met, and where it was presented, but I'm sure we enjoyed it. After all, a play given by the University of Pennsylvania young men would be wonderful in our eyes.

Sun. Dec. 5 – Frank & Isobel stayed overnight. A Miss Roberts came up. Fooled around in afternoon. Arrived back very tired.

Frank and Isobel often came up and spent part of a weekend with us. I think he often came because he loved my mother's apple pie.

My father's students were called "Brother or Sister." This guest was a newcomer and was still called by the name Miss. I do not remember what she looked like, or very much about her, but she became an important, though damaging, part of my father's life. Suffice here to say she was partially responsible for his being removed from his position a few years later.

Tues – Dec. 7 – Nothing much happened. Had Algebra test. Just vile! Flunked.

Wed. – Dec. 8 – Got 75 in Algebra. What a surprise.

Am on food committee for children's party Sat.

That mark in Algebra must have been a big load off my mind. I loved my father very much, even though some of the things he had done to me in the past were perplexing, but sometimes I was afraid of him. Getting poor marks in school was one of those times, so even though this 75 in Algebra was not great, at least it was passing. He knew I was not good in mathematics of any kind. Once more I was obtaining my goal – keep my Dad happy with me.

Fri. Dec 10 – A year since Edward abdicated. Had A.A. party in evening. Quite good, play, candy, etc.

I see I'm still showing my British heritage. Now I'm on a more personal basis remembering King Edward VIII's Abdication, for he is now just Edward.

Again, I'm up against trying to decipher what I wrote 70 years ago, but I'm pretty sure that an A.A. party was not one put on by Alcoholics Anonymous but rather our Athletic Association.

Sat. Dec. 11 – Finished ping-pong tournament. Limy won & got a lovely gold cup. Mu Sigma gave a party for 20 poor kids. Fun. Gave them candy & ice cream & games. Got announcement of conference reunion.

And here I thought I was a pretty good ping-pong player. I remember Limy. Her read name was Jean Lyman and she was one of my close friends.

Mu Sigma was the school honor society. I don't remember too much about this party, but apparently it was an annual event. I don't know how the children were chosen, but I'm sure they enjoyed being driven out of downtown Stamford to the elegant-looking Shippan Point, and joining the girls of Low-Heywood in a fun afternoon. Hope they liked the food I had helped arrange for them.

The conference reunion was for those of us who'd attended the church conference this past summer, and who lived in the New York area. I wasn't sure whether or not my parents would allow me to attend, for they might assume that Ted would be there. I suppose if he was and I saw him, in that case it would be okay to say hello.

Sun. Dec 12 – Piano recital. Christmas carol service. Very nice. Spoke to Miss Tilley about calling Mother about going to reunion. She said to write a special delivery. Wrote it. Here's hoping.

This entry intrigues me. I wonder why I involved Miss Tilley in what was not even a school-related happening. I'm wondering, too, why I was begging with my mother to let me go to the conference reunion instead of with my dad. Possibly he was out of town and they needed an answer soon on how many were going to attend. In those days we would rarely call someone long distance, especially for a "not-so-important" question as this one represented. Obviously it was very important to me, as I was willing to spend the extra postage and send her a special delivery letter. I had wanted to call her, but Miss Tilley, for some unknown reason, suggested this means of communication.

Tues. Dec. 13 – Waited for telephone from Mother but she didn't call. Very worried. My bed was damp so Miss Muchenfurs helped me make the bed over.

How dramatic can a teenager get – to be so worried over a yes or no answer.

I have no idea who Miss Muchernfurs was or why my bed was wet. I sure hope it was because of a spilled glass of water and not for some other reason.

Tues. Dec. 14 – Mother called up at 8 A.M. & said I could go to the reunion. Shouted all over the place.

Oh what simple things brought joy to a seventeen-year old in 1937.

Thurs. Dec. 16 – Pageant. Went caroling in evening. Fun. Went around Shippan point & landed up at Miss Roper's for cookies & cake. Packed.

Each year some of the girls put on a Christmas pageant. I don't recall that I was in any of them, and I'm guessing it was usually members of the Dramatic Club who participated.

As I have mentioned, Shippan Point was one of the nicer residential areas of Stamford. I'm sure the occupants were used to the Low-Heywood girls caroling under their windows each year. I thought it was a very nice thing we did.

Miss Roper's home was adjacent to the front of the Main Building, and easily accessible for us when we came back tired and, possibly, a bit cold. It was rarely that any of us were allowed in her home, for if we were being reprimanded for anything, it would always occur either in the school office, or in an empty classroom.

Fri. Dec. 17 – Gave Miss Waldo a picture for Christmas. She was so nice about it. Arrived home. Dad gave me $5. Pajama case from Auntie Brookfield.

Most of us had crushes on some of the teachers. I know I dallied back and forth, one year liking a certain one, and the following year I couldn't stand her. This held true for Miss Waldo, our history teacher.

Looking back I remember her as a typical "old-maid" teacher. She was not too tall, had gray hair piled on top of her head held there with combs, wore pinz-nez glasses on a black satin ribbon around her neck, and spit when she talked (we'd make fun of her doing this behind her back), but on the whole a nice person. This was the year when I felt close to her, and so I gave her a present for Christmas. I do not recall what the picture was.

Mary Brookfield was an associate of my father when he worked in England. She was no relation to me, other than the fact she was my godmother, but I had always called her Auntie Brookie. When I grew older and liked to imagine romantic scenarios, I often wondered if my dad was "taken with her," and perhaps my being called Mary was not only for my mother, but also for her. She later became one of the persons honored by the King and made a Member of the Order of the British Empire. I still have the letter she wrote me describing in detail what the ceremony was like.

Tues. Dec. 21 – Went to the dentist. Everything O.K. Mother & I saw "Second Honeymoon" & "Victoria the Great." Good. Wrapped Christmas presents up & fixed the manger.

So many things fascinate me as I re-write these early years. I now wonder why I wrote the obvious second-rate movie "Second Honeymoon," first in the order of movies we saw, and "Victoria the Great," with the actress Ann Neagle, the story of which has been produced in film and on stage, many times. It's possible that, since the latter film was about history, and at this point I was fed up with all kinds of history, I thought having a second honeymoon much more delightful.

I don't remember where I got the manger, which I set up each year. All the figures were cream-colored. As a young girl I used it for many years, and then when my children arrived they helped me set it up. I still have it. Recently I gave it to one of my sons for his family to use.

Sat. Dec. 25 – Christmas Day. Got gloves, sport socks, slippers, Yardley's set, bath set, bath powder, slips, cookies, candy, weave set, scarf. Got a nice stocking from Frank & Isobel. Said from Snooty. Goose for lunch.

Looks like this was a pretty good Christmas for me. Sure hope no one swiped this Yardley set. Maybe I had sense enough to leave it at home for my use there.

Copying Mr. Dickens and the Cratchit family, we were still very British in having goose for Christmas dinner. I never did foist that upon my family, though I did occasionally serve duck.

Tues. Dec. 28 – Reunion dinner. Met Audrey for lunch. Ate at a Chinese restaurant. Saw Ted – was only polite to him. I don't like him anymore. Saw Beth. Am going on a double date with Audrey New Years.

And so I attended the famous reunion about which I previously was in such a panic. After all that "emotional commotion" I inflicted upon myself, it doesn't seem to have made much of an impression on me, or at least not enough to enter into my diary. I am amused at my comment about Ted. Life goes on, and our views change. As I look back on this episode, I just wish my parents, or at least my dad, had stayed out of the picture and let me work this out for myself. Obviously when I met him again six months later, I no longer liked him.

Fri. Dec. 31 - Went to Audrey's & stayed overnight. Slept with her sister. Went on a double date with a fellow named Bill, Aud & Ev. Saw "Wells Fargo" in N.Y.C. Crowd. Swell. Eats after. Home at 4.

This entry really surprises me that my dad allowed me to do this. He thought a lot of Audrey and, because she was a year older than I was, I presume felt she was capable of taking care of me. As I have mentioned several times in these pages, moral standards in the 1930s were extremely high. No one I associated with ever openly talked about sex or doing something with a guy. It just didn't enter our heads to discuss this, as no one we knew ever succumbed. Therefore, Dad would assume rightly that we were just going on a date – dinner, a show, and the mad, mad crowd in Times Square on New Year's Eve. And this is exactly what happened.

I recall the first year when we were reunited as a family in the United States, we ventured into Times Square on that New Years Eve 1929. It was crowded, it was noisy, it was tumultuous and this night, with Audrey and friends, was the only other time I ever succumbed to enter into this pandemonium. I lived in the general area for several years, and for the last eight years before I married, I actually lived in New York City, but I never again went there on New Years Eve. Earlier I'd listen to all the goings-on, on the radio, later watch it on TV, and fondly remember the date I had in 1937.

~The End~

February 2011. Publisher's note:

Mary's diary covers five years: 1935 through 1939. All five volumes, one for each year, are available on Kindle as well as attractive paperback books.
You may also want to read more of Mary's prize winning stories on our website. Or try some of the over 1,000 other stories you'll find there by authors from all over the world. Go to www.storyhouse.org and enjoy our commercial free web site dedicated to "preserving the extraordinary works of 'ordinary' people."

Richard Loller, Publisher,
The Preservation Foundation, Inc.
A Not-For-Profit Publisher
richard@storyhouse.org

Made in the USA
Middletown, DE
22 June 2020